The Pavilion Book

Sacramento, California

The Pavilion Book

A guide to Buying, Maintaining, and Living in a Medieval—style Tent

With a special section on

Tentmaking Tips, Tools, and Techniques

John LaTorre

With illustrations and photographs by the author

Sacramento, California

I believe that the best students are also teachers, and that the best teachers will always be students. Therefore, I dedicate this book to all my teachers, and all my students.

Special thanks to Peter C. Barclay and Sunny Hara for ferreting out most of the mistakes in the manuscript, suggesting re-wording where I wasn't clear, and giving me the benefit of their own considerable experience in camping and tentmaking.

Thanks also to Tanya Clapshaw and Adam MacDonald for their help and encouragement over the years, and to my wife Debra for all she is.

© 2006, by John LaTorre

All rights reserved. No part of this book may be reproduced in any form, except for brief reviews, without the written permission of the author.

ISBN 978-0-9790635-0-3

First Printing

Published by Dragonwing
P. O. Box 13322, Sacramento, California 95813-3322

Table of Contents

Introduction

There have been hundreds of books on camping (with or without tents) and more than a few on the Society for Creative Anachronism, Inc., but this is the first one about the ins and outs of camping in period pavilions. I've written it because a tent is a big investment in money (if you're buying one) or time and money (if you're making one), and you want to get the best value for your investment.

Nearly every one of the techniques, tips, and strategies mentioned in this book comes from my own personal experience, augmented by observations from people whose advice I've come to trust. I've spent over thirty years putting pieces of cloth together, first as a sailmaker specializing in aviation sails (for hang gliders and ultralight aircraft) and then as a tentmaker. And with over forty years of camping (twenty of them in the SCA), I've learned a bit about using outdoor shelters. Now that knowledge is yours, too!

(In the course of this book I'll be primarily discussing the SCA, which is the world's largest organization devoted to medieval study and re-creation activities, because that's where I play nowadays. But the information will also be valuable, to a greater or lesser extent, for other re-creationist groups such as the Empire of Chivalry and Steel, the Adrian Empire, and various English Civil War groups, and a multitude of others. The differences among these groups are primarily in the degree of authenticity they demand and the necessary compromises you need to make in order to satisfy those demands. If you're participating in one of these venues, it's important to find out what those standards are before investing in equipment. But because you still have to set it up, transport it, and live in it, there's still a lot of useful stuff here.)

Re-creation camping is different from other kinds of camping in one crucial respect. I like to think of us as a theater in which we are all actors in one role or another. Our camping environment is our set, and we are all set designers and builders as well as actors, costumers, caterers, and scriptwriters. As backdrops to the event, our tents are an essential part of that theater set, as indispensable as the costumes and the pageantry.

People often ask me how to furnish their camp in "period" style, and what styles of furniture would be applicable to which periods. This is a thornier question than it first appears, because it presumes that people in period camped like we do in the SCA. In fact, they didn't camp out at all as a rule, except for specific purposes. The celebrated "Field of the Cloth of Gold," for instance, was a summit meeting where the tents were used for exhibitions and negotiating sessions; there's no indication that anybody slept in them. The usual routine when nobles were traveling was to put them up in whatever houses were handy, usually displacing the inhabitants who, in their turn, displaced the people who were sleeping in the barns. (The people displaced from the barns slept wherever they could, but probably not in tents.) We know that tents were extensively used in military campaigns, for which fact we are indebted because the vast majority of our tent depictions come from scenes of battles and sieges.

Tents were also used as arming pavilions in tournaments, but again, there's no indication that they were anything but temporary day shelters, dressing areas and storage areas.

About the only way we might see a medieval depiction of camping that's remotely like ours is when viewing paintings intended to depict, say, an encampment mentioned in a Bible story. In a hypothetical painting of the *Camp of the Israelites in the Desert* by the equally hypothetical Otto von Schnurrbartfarbe, you might find nobility in tents surrounded by all the drapes and furniture and other good things in their lives. But bear in mind that the artist was portraying not an actual medieval situation but his conception of a Biblical one using the medieval artifacts he was familiar with. Similarly, when we sleep and entertain in our tents, even if we take great pains to have our tents and furniture historically correct, we probably look a lot more like a scene in old Otto's imagination than any scene he might have seen with his own eyes.

Of course, most of the camps you see in the SCA, with their mix of Viking tents and yurts and Renaissance rounds, look a lot weirder than anything Otto ever could ever have imagined. So unless they're really trying for a single-focus encampment, SCAdians don't worry overmuch about every detail being correct. There are, of course, other historical re-creation organizations that have stricter levels of authenticity than the SCA, but those that participate in them should be aware that in most of their contexts, the "Period Medieval" encampment would never have existed at all. The point is that whatever we're attempting to re-enact, the re-enactment works better if we pay attention to what it is supposed to look like, and how it's supposed to advance the purpose of the re-creation.

Aside from their function as backdrops to the theater, tents serve the additional purpose of protection, as important to your health and safety as the armor that the fighters wear. Like a suit of armor, a tent is designed to be beautiful and authentic-looking, but its real value lies in its ability to protect you from those elements that want to do you ill. And while only fighters need protection from blows, everybody needs protection from the weather. (And I hardly need to mention that you'll spend a lot more time in your tent than any fighter spends in his or her armor.)

So for most people, a tent is *the* major purchase of their hobby, even if it's not necessarily the one they spend the most money on.

That said, a "period" tent might not be the best tent for you. There's no question that a modern tent costs less and is easier to transport and assemble. The very best of them are almost as comfortable as period pavilions of comparable size, and there are tricks you can use to make even the most uncomfortable of them a little more habitable. I must confess here that I have used a modern tent from time to time, when I had limited cargo space and not enough time to set up my usual encampment. There's no shame attached. (At least, I didn't feel much shame, which may not be the same thing).

But if you're willing to cope with a few disadvantages in pursuit of the goal of making the "theater set" more attractive, a period tent is worth the trouble – particularly if you want to be close to the action, because in many SCA venues, the more period the tent, the closer you can camp to the focal points of the event.

Of course, buying a tent is only the first step. There are a multitude of tricks to make it more comfortable, weather-resistant, and useful. As I mentioned earlier, I've learned a few of them in the course of forty years of camping, over twenty of them in the SCA. During those twenty years, I've also been a professional tentmaker who's made hundreds of tents, in a wide range of sizes, for customers all over the country. These customers have been quick to tell me what worked and what didn't, and they've shared an eternally fascinating stream of information on how they use their tents in their re-enactment activities.

This book is the result, and I dedicate it to them, and to all the people who've participated in my tent and camping seminars.

PART ONE: Buying and Maintaining a Tent

in which is explained the arts of acquiring a tent, making it last longer, and keeping it clean

1. Buying a Tent

Since buying a tent involves plunking down an impressive amount of money, you want to know how to get the best value for that investment, regardless of which manufacturer you buy it from. That's what this chapter is about.

I haven't bought many tents in my life, but I've sold quite a few, and I've seen people make good choices and bad choices in what they selected. The people that were happiest with their purchases were always the ones that carefully assessed their needs and camping styles, instead of buying the biggest tent they could afford.

Try before you buy

This is Rule Number One. I always recommend that before you buy a tent, you find somebody with a similar tent and ask them if you could watch them set it up and take it down. Even better, ask if you can help. Find out what they like about the tent, and what they don't. See how many people it takes, and how much time it takes. Imagine what it would be like to set it up a couple of dozen times in a variety of weather conditions.

One of the advantages of huge events like Lilies, Pennsic War or Estrella War is that you get to see a lot of different styles of tents and talk with a huge number of owners. Chances are that somebody there has a tent like the one you're intending to buy, and can offer sage advice and counsel.

How Much Tent?

If you're always camping with a large household, it makes sense to buy a large tent. You'll need it for entertaining when the weather's bad. But buying a big tent under the impression that it works for any number of people from one to n is a mistake, for two reasons:

- If you're the only one going to a particular event, you're stuck with setting up that large tent by yourself, or leaving it at home and taking the dome tent instead.
- If there are a lot of people in your group, and you expect to accommodate both entertaining in the tent and sleeping everybody inside, those two needs are going to have to be juggled.

The system that seems to work best for group camping is one larger under-canvas area (which in the SCA's West Kingdom is usually a sunshade rather than an enclosed tent) used for entertaining, with several small personal tents providing the sleeping quarters. The sunshade itself is often segmented; if there are not going to be many people at the event who need the shelter, only one segment is used, but for larger, longer events, two or three can be linked together. So unless you're buying tentage for the entire household, you're better off with a smaller tent for your personal use. Smaller tents take less time to set up and strike, freeing time for other things. And they're easier to transport.

What Size?

Deciding the right size tent for your needs is tricky, because people vary in their comfort levels and in the amount of stuff they carry around. An absolute minimum would be about 12 square feet per person, which is just about enough room to stretch out and sleep. To accommodate camping supplies, clothing, and the like, it's better to figure twenty to twenty-five square feet per person. Double that if you're a fighter or bring lots of other toys with you. The longer the event, the more room you will need for any degree of comfort.

If you go to many events where the amount of space you're allotted is limited, you have to take that into account, as well. That's another situation where it makes sense to have very small tents for sleeping and a shared area for socializing and cooking.

The size that works best for my wife and me is about a hundred square feet. That gives us enough room to set up a double bed (with storage underneath), a chair, and a card table inside the tent and still have floor space for dressing and maneuvering. We also have room to take in the travel harp and spinning wheel and store them under the table at night. We've entertained four or five people comfortably in the tent (including ourselves) by seating two on the bed and bringing in chairs from outside, but it was tight; if we wanted to have more room for entertaining, a 150 square foot tent might be a better choice. An even larger tent would allow us to bring in our dining table, but we keep that outside, under the sunshade.

What Shape?

This is another area of contention, with so many several variables that making categorical recommendations is impossible. These variables include historical authenticity, cost, ease of transport, ease of set-up, useable space, and comfort. And, as I'll explain shortly, tents vary in the ratio of their "footprint" (the area they take up, including ropes) to the useable space they provide.

I have a particular axe to grind here. I believe that the more serious we are about re-creating an authentic environment as a backdrop for our activities, we more obliged we are to stick with the shapes that predominated during the Middle Ages. These shapes are the conical tents, round tents, and oval tents. The fact that we can find the occasional square tent or wedge tent in period depictions justifies the use of these other shapes to a degree, but when an encampment has a preponderance of square and rectangular tents, it ceases to look like an authentic medieval encampment. Imagine a movie, set in the 1970s in Salt Lake City, where everybody is dressed in bell-bottoms and mini-skirts, and you'll see what I mean.

I am admittedly in the minority here, because many (if not most) people are more comfortable in tents with a square or rectangular floor plan. It's easier to fit furniture in the corners, and the structures holding them up are usually less complicated. And when your tent has a flat front profile, it's easier to attach an awning to it. Generally, the smaller the tent is, the more efficient the square or rectangular shape is over the round varieties; the larger the tent is, the less difference it makes. Your choice also depends on how seriously you take your "persona." For some folks, it's not a big issue. They just want a tent that's reasonably period-looking, regardless of whether a person from their culture would have been caught dead in one. Others, who like to camp in areas dedicated to a certain historical culture, find an accurate tent to be indispensable to their games.

Figure 1. Conical Tent

Your choices range from a conical tent with a single center pole to elaborate hub-and-spoke ovals. The conical tent, with its single pole, gives you the ultimate simplicity of frame, at the expense of not much headroom in comparison to its footprint. You also see square versions of this tent; they look like elongated pyramids.

The pyramid tent, with a square or rectangular footprint, is also the easiest to set up. You simply stake down the four corners (making sure the door is closed on the bottom). Then you drive in the intermediate stakes, if any, and raise the pole, and you're done. With a conical tent, the process is slightly more complex, because you have to make sure that the circle isn't distorted. It helps to use a fitted ground cloth to help locate the stakes here.

The next step up from that is what is usually called a "bell wedge" or "French Bell" tent, consisting of two center poles, a

9

ridge pole, and maybe a couple of poles for an attached awning (which is optional in fair weather but practically mandatory in rainy weather, if you want to keep the door area dry). It characteristically has the look of an oversized pup tent familiar to those in the Army, but with

Figure 2. Bell Wedge Tent

the door set in the central flat area and with rounded ends. (A variation of this is the getheld, which also employs two center poles and a ridge pole, but puts the ridge pole through a sleeve sewn to the top of the tent, and situates the tent's doors at the ends rather than in the central flat area.) For this increased structure, you get a bit more useable floor area, a little more headroom, and the ability to hang things off the ridgepole. This style finds many advocates, particularly among people who don't have much room in their vehicles to transport a lot of poles. It's also easy to set up, particularly if there's a fitted ground cloth so you know where to stake the sides down; it's just a question of putting in the stakes and raising the frame inside the tent.

Figure 3. Viking Tent

Another variant of the wedge is the Viking tent, which also has the pup-tent shape, but differs in its structure. It consists of two rigid triangles at each end connected by a ridgepole and base poles. Some historians think that this frame accommodated a sail (or other large fabric piece) draped over the ridgepole and connected to the base pole. It's a very stable shape, with the advantage that the finished tent can be picked up and re-located when necessary, but it has much more structure than the other wedge styles and is correspondingly harder to transport and set up.

Here's a point about all the above-mentioned tents that often escapes notice: the bigger they are, the better they work. All these tents suffer from a relative paucity of headroom, but the larger ones have correspondingly more of this commodity. There are some things you just can't effectively scale down, particularly if you insist in having furniture like beds inside, but also want to have some floor space with standing room as well.

The next step up from these tents is what I'll call Roman-style wall tents. These also have two or three center poles and a ridge pole, but have roofs that don't go all the way to the ground but are connected to low walls. The eaves are supported by ropes, often truncated through the use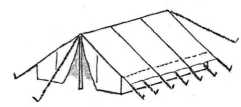

Figure 4. Roman Wall Tent

of smaller poles supporting the eaves. Again, the larger these are, the more effective headroom they provide. This style has been around more or less continuously since the era of imperial Rome, but wasn't extensively used in the Middle Ages, from what we can see from depictions. It works best when set up in rows of similar tents, since the guy ropes of adjoining tents can share the same space, thus using the available camping space more efficiently.

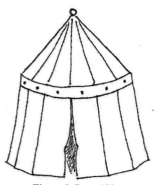

Figure 5. Round Tent

The most prevalent tent shapes in the Middle Ages were the round tents and oval tents (also called oblong tents, or round-end marquees), with well-defined eaves and walls that hang more vertically than the roof panels. I'll try to head off some lexicographic confusion here by explaining that many people call any sort of round tent a "bell" tent, regardless of whether or not it has the abovementioned well-defined eaves, but for the purposes of this book, round tents have eaves and true bell tents don't.

I'm also going to lump the square versions of these defined-eave tents into this category, since the frames are quite similar.

I've seen (and built) more types of supports for this sort of tent than I can shake a stick at. The historical record is of no help whatsoever here, since no period references have been found to describe these supports, and period depictions don't show them (although they seem to indicate that some form of structure must have been used). So we're forced to be creative in our approach to this challenge.

The simplest version uses a center pole, with ropes radiating out from the eaves and staked down sufficiently far out from the eave that the rope alone supports the eave. The drawback, of course, is that tents of any size occupy a footprint three or four times the area of the tent's floor space. And this set-up requires more attention to keeping the ropes adequately tensioned, so the walls don't sag. But it's unquestionably period.

Figure 6. Hub-and-spoke tent

The next iteration relies on a center pole with the eaves supported by either a rigid ring or (in the square versions of this tent, horizontal eave poles) or a hub-and-spoke arrangement; in the latter arrangement, the eave is supported by struts radiating out from the center pole. Either one works well, and results in a greatly reduced (or even non-existent) rope radius. Having built round pavilions with both styles in several versions, I've come to the conclusion that for tents less than ten foot (three meters) in diameter at the eave, rings are a more efficient structure (in the sense of what you get versus what it weighs), while tents of a greater eave diameter would do well to go with a spoke arrangement instead. If your eave radius is right at ten feet, you could go either way.

The rings don't need to be single piece. All the ones I've made have been segmented and break down into component pieces of four or five feet, which are easy to transport. In theory, there isn't any limit to the number of segments that can

Figure 7. Ring tether

be created, although if the ring has angles bent into it to accommodate the shape of the canopy's eave, the splices should be between the bends, not at them.

After years of making round tents, I've found out that the bigger ones really need to have some sort of eave stabilization system, to keep the eave from moving with respect to the center pole. The hub-and-spoke system offers this feature automatically, but tents with rings can accomplish this by using ropes to tether the ring to the center pole. I do this by providing six or eight eye-bolts on the rings, corresponding eye-screws on the center pole, and hooks on the ends of each rope segment. This arrangement works much the same as the spokes on a bicycle wheel, operating under tension rather than compression. It provides the same stability and offers you most of the same opportunities as the spokes for hanging stuff, storing things overhead, and so on, but at a small fraction of the weight.

A third option is to support the eave with side poles. This system, in fact comes standard with most of the square varieties of eave-defined tents. It works well, but you really take a licking in weight, since the poles are much heavier than an equivalent arrangement of spokes or ring segments. If you go this route, you're one step away from the ultimate in round tent structures: eliminating the center pole entirely, and supporting the roof shape with a separate structure (usually incorporating a strut-supported "false" center pole) that rests on the tops of the side poles. I made a few tents this way, but found that the convenience of an open floor area really didn't justify the added weight and set-up complexity. (None of the bigger tentmakers offers this set-up as an option, and this may be why.) But for some people with unusual floor-space requirements, such as large pieces of furniture, this sort of structure may be an option as a retrofit.

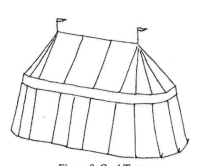

Figure 8. Oval Tent

After round tents come the oval or oblong tents. Structurally, they can be seen as "stretched" rounds. Like "stretch" aircraft, which are made by dropping in central sections of varying lengths to a basic fuselage design, they're what you get when you cut a round tent in two vertically, separate the sections an appropriate amount, and insert fabric in between to cover the gap. They usually have two or three center poles, a ridgepole, and the same sort of eave supports you see in round tents. The advantage is that you have a large central area largely unencumbered by poles, and separate areas in the rounded ends that can be concealed by drapes for privacy. But you pay for that in added structure and weight.

The square defined-eave tent has its counterpart in the large rectangular tent, often called a "marquee" tent. The eaves of these tents are almost invariably supported by side poles.

Finally, there are styles that don't fit any of the preceding categories, but which have their adherents. These include yurts (also called gers), Quonset-hut configurations, market umbrella conversions, portable carport conversions, Bedouin tents, and so on. I'm not going to cover them here, because I frankly don't have a lot of experience with them. (In particular, there's already an excellent book called *The Complete Yurt Handbook*, by Paul King, which covers that particular style in exhaustive detail.) The trade-off for all these is that they don't always fit in the context of the medieval environment that you are trying to re-create. But they may work for your circumstances.

Choosing a Fabric

The only other big difference between commercially available tents is in the fabric used. There are two categories of choices: flame-retardant vs. non-flame retardant, and all-cotton vs. cotton/polyester.

Flame-retardant or not?

If you're buying the tent in California (and a few other states), you're going to be getting a flame-retardant tent if your supplier is operating within the law. Otherwise, it's your choice. But you should be aware that if you intend to use the tent in circumstances like SCA merchanting, Renaissance Faires or the like, the operators (or the local authorities) may require that the tent be flame-retardant, and they will ask for proof in the form of documentation from the manufacturer. And a flame-retardant tent may be easier to sell down the road, since it will increase the pool of potential customers to include merchants and RenFaire people.

When I started making tents commercially in California, I had to conform to the legal requirement that all tents made in California, or sold in California, be made of flame-retardant material. I used to chafe at this requirement, because it severely limited me in the choice of fabrics I could use and the price I had to pay for them. Over the years, my thinking has changed somewhat. What has changed my mind more than anything else is seeing very large SCA encampments, sometimes stretching for miles, with tents pitched extremely close together. As of this writing, there hasn't been a major fire, but I think now that it's only a question of time. A few Pennsics back, a fire broke out near the camp, and disaster was averted only because the wind was blowing the flames away from the camp and not toward it. And those of you who were at the SCA's Thirty-Year Celebration will remember what a fire-trap that was, with closely-pitched tents surrounded by freshly cut hay. I'm now convinced that it is a Good Thing to have sleeping areas be flame-retardant.

Don't assume that the tent you buy will be flame-retardant. Most of the major manufacturers are pretty good about complying with the law, but there are smaller ones, even in California, whose tents are not flame-retardant. If you buy one of these tents, you are not protected. Inquire of the manufacturer whether the tent is truly made of flame-retardant fabric as required by law. They should be able to show some documentation that the tent conforms to California's CPAI-84 specification (which is the most stringent and therefore the one that everybody else uses, too). Also, be aware that most Renaissance Faires have a requirement that the tents used there be flame-retardant, of if you plan on participating in these venues, you may need to show some documentation.

All Cotton, Some Cotton, or No Cotton?

The most popular all-cotton fabric is something called Sunforger (actually a trademark of MF&H Textiles, Butler, Georgia for the finishing process of the cloth, but more commonly applied to the tight-weave canvas cloth finished using the process). It is much more expensive than most types of cotton canvas, but cheaper than cotton/polyester canvas. In tentage form, it comes preshrunk and treated for water-repellence and mildew resistance. A flame-retardant version can also be had, at a higher cost.

Then there are all-cotton "duck" canvases. The term isn't very helpful, since it is bandied about fairly indiscriminately to connote any heavy, densely woven cotton cloth. Some of it is good for tents, particularly if it's been pre-shrunk or otherwise stabilized. You'll have to rely on the tent manufacturer's reputation here, rather than the description of the cloth.

There's no question that cotton/polyester tentage fabric is a lot more expensive than all-cotton fabric, but its superior longevity and its ability to dry quickly make it the material of choice for many people. It also comes in a dozen different colors, making it easy to achieve a colorful tent without painting it. When people ask me whether the additional cost is worth it, I remind them of the situation you face when you're having the house painted; buying the best paint you can will save you money in the long run, because labor is expensive and you don't want to pay for it twice when, with better paint, the job would have lasted twice as long. Again, the choice is yours. If you have the space to hang up a wet tent indoors to dry thoroughly before you store it, if you promise to never, never, never store it wet, and you don't expect to be using the tent very much, an all-cotton fabric may serve your needs well. Make sure that the fabric is designed for tents. It should be of a tight weave and be treated for mildew resistance and water repellence.

I suppose I should mention other synthetic woven cloths like *Sunbrella* (a trademark of Raven Mills). They are often lighter and more durable than the two previous cloths I mentioned, but they are considerably more expensive. And as far as I know, no manufacture of "period" pavilions is using it on a regular basis, so it's not a choice that you're likely to be offered. It's also worth mentioning that many awning fabrics are not designed for repeated folding and unfolding, which makes them undesirable for tents.

Bells and Whistles

There are a few other choices you may have on what you get with your tent. Here's a rundown on some of the more popular options:

Sod Flaps. These are typically extensions to the bottom wall. Originally, they were used to help seal out running ground water. A portion of the sod was removed along the outer perimeter of the tent, the flaps were tucked into the hole, and the sod replaced (see Figure 9A). Used like this, they do an excellent job of keeping the interior of the tent dry.

Unfortunately, many of the campgrounds we use don't allow

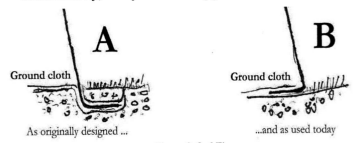

Ground cloth

A

As originally designed ...

Ground cloth

B

...and as used today

Figure 9. Sod Flaps

us to dig up the sod. So the sod flaps are used instead in conjunction with a ground cloth (as shown in Figure 9B) to help seal the bottom of the tents from drafts and such. In this function, they work well. They really don't do much against keeping water out of the tent, though.

Do you need them? It usually depends on how much cold-weather camping you expect to do, or what sort of fauna you usually share your campground with. They usually complicate set-up slightly, but compensate by helping to seal the bottom of the tent against drafts and crawling critters.

Ground cloths. You need at least a rudimentary form of ground cloth, of course, to keep the moisture in the ground from coming up into the tent. For this function, it need only be a thin plastic or vinyl sheet. But the thicker it is, the longer it will wear, and the more resistant to punctures it will be, so if you're often camping on rocky ground instead of lawns, a thicker plastic will be money well spent.

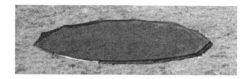

Figure 10. Fitted Ground Cloth With Lip

My favorite kind of ground cloth is the one with a three-inch lip, supported by its own little stakes. It is custom-fitted to the tent and provides a positive protection against standing water that accumulates when it's raining harder than the ground can absorb. Its disadvantages are extra weight and cost, and an additional tripping hazard when the lip is deployed (although the lip is usually lowered and tucked under the edge of the carpet when the weather is fair). People have snickered when I spread out and staked my "portable koi pond," but it's kept the contents of the tent dry after cloudbursts that left an inch of standing water all around the tent.

Separate sidewalls vs. single-piece construction. With smaller tents, it's not an issue, but with the larger ones, it makes more sense to have detachable sides, because more pieces that weigh less individually are easier to transport, pack, and store than one gigantic piece that weighs a lot. Those without a lot of body strength will appreciate this feature. It's also possible to drop or fold back portions of the sides (depending on the design of the tent) in warm weather to allow cross-ventilation.

Slanted sidewalls vs. vertical sidewalls. Sides that slant outward are somewhat more stable in winds, because the air can be induced to travel over the tent rather than having to push into it. The more slanted the walls are, the greater this effect. There's a bonus in that tents with walls having a generous slant (say, twenty degrees or more from vertical) require no guy ropes; the walls themselves act as guying mechanisms, saving you some time and hassle. If you go this route, though, remember that

17

once the walls become integral parts of the structure, they can't be peeled back, dropped, or removed when it gets warm, so you have to either provide some other sort of ventilation or be able to substitute a guy rope for the cloth as needed. At the very least, the tent should have a front door and back door that provide some cross-ventilation when opened.

Closures. Your choice here is between zippers, ties, and some sort of loop-and-toggle or loop-and-hook arrangement. Zippers, of course, are definitely out of period, although many people order them for their unrivalled convenience. When offered for medieval tents, the zippers are usually concealed by gussets so they don't grate on your senses. About all the advice I can give you here is that if you go this route, you want a large zipper (a #5 or, even better, a #10) separating zipper with a double-toggle slide rather than the garment-size zipper found on most commercial tents. They are far more robust and trouble-free.

Most tents offer ties as a standard closure, and they work well. The only differences between manufacturers are the spacing and the material of the ties. I think that the ties should be spaced no more than about two feet apart, and people who camp in windy conditions might appreciate a closer spacing. The wider the door overlap, the wider the spacing of the ties can be. One factor that's often overlooked is how the ties behave when wet ... some swell to the point where untying knots can be almost impossible, and others (mainly those of synthetic webbing) don't take knots at all. All of the manufactured tents I've seen have acceptable ties, but you see a lot of homebuilt ones that don't.

The last category is the one where toggles or hooks on one side of the door engage with loops on the other side. These have the benefit of being easier to fasten than ties, but they don't make quite as positive a seal and are often slightly more expensive to fit.

Stake loops. Almost every tent has sides that require staking to the ground, and the loops that the stakes go through get a lot of abuse. In my experience, the most trouble-free arrangement is a solid steel ring (either round or D-shaped), attached to the sidewall by a loop of webbing. My second choice would be a rope loop that goes through a grommet or other reinforcement in the bottom of the sidewall. These loops should not be sewn onto the cloth, but should be easily replaceable in the field with similar rope.

Next come loops made with webbing or fabric, sewn onto the skirt of the sidewall. These seem to be the most prevalent setup by far on commercial tents, but I don't like them because they wear out and require periodic replacement. The last option is large grommets in the skirt of the tent through which the stakes go. My basic gripe with these is that they put the cloth directly in contact with the ground, causing it to wick moisture from the soil. The grommets themselves also take a beating, especially when the occasional hammer blow misses the stake and strikes the grommet itself.

Windows and vents. If you're camping in hot weather, these become almost essential in some styles of tents, particularly those where the sidewalls of the tent are sewn to the canopy. They vary from simple slits near the peak that can be covered with a flap when the weather is inclement all the way to elaborate windows with screening. If you're ordering a tent, they're worth the added expense, particularly since they're much easier to install when the roof is in pieces than afterwards, when the roof is a single piece. They increase the "fiddle factor" when setting up or using the tent, but most people find that they can live with this drawback. Not all manufacturers offer this option, since they can't be confident that the windows or vents will be used properly and don't want to take the blame if rain penetrates the flap and gets inside the tent.

If you have tents with sidewalls that detach, you may not need vents, since you can drop portions of the walls to allow cross-ventilation. Some designs do this better than others, so it's worth asking around to see what other people's experiences have been, and whether they've had to compromise some measure of privacy to achieve comfort.

Colored cloth. If you're buying a tent from a factory that offers colored cloth, you can get as artistic as you want with the sidewalls and the valance. But I would recommend against going with a dark roof for several reasons:

- A white roof lasts longer because it reflects more of the sun's ultraviolet rays than dark cloth does, resulting in less UV damage over time. It also tends to be stronger in the first place, since many dying processes result in weakening the cloth slightly. (This is particularly true of very dark or black cloth. One of the dirty little secrets of the textile business is that a lot of black cloth has been subjected to two dying processes. If a cloth comes out the wrong color in the initial dying, the cloth finisher finds it very tempting to re-dye it black rather than have to sell off the cloth as seconds.)
- A white roof lets you get more light from your lamps at night, particularly if you hang them high enough to allow the roof's fabric to act as a reflector.
- At sunset, a white roof gives you about fifteen more minutes to find your candles, lanterns, and matches.

About the only reason I can think of for going with a dark roof is if you happen to be very sensitive to UV radiation, and require that the roof stop as much of that radiation as it can. For most people, it's not a problem.

Buying a Used Tent

As with buying anything used (or "pre-owned," as the auto industry likes to put it), you can get great deals on the one hand, or badly burned on the other. Before you commit yourself, look over the assembled, erected tent with a cold dispassionate eye. Has it stretched overmuch anywhere? Is any of the fabric worn, frayed, or ripped? Ask if you can give the cloth a "knuckle test" where you tension a bit of the cloth (like on an embroidery frame) and attempt to force the knuckle of your folded-over index finger through the fabric. If there is a small tear anywhere, see how much effort it takes to get the tear to continue, and read the chapter on tent repairs to see what it's going to take to do a proper repair.

Look at the poles. Were they ever given a coat of finish? How is the finish on them holding up? Are they straight? If they're much more than a diameter out of column, their strength is compromised. What shape are the hardware, ropes, and fittings in?

No used tent is likely to be in absolutely perfect condition. That's why you're getting a deal on it, right? But it's worth remembering that a tent is essentially like a disposable razor or cigarette lighter or ballpoint pen. Its lifetime is finite, and the time will come when it's used up and not worth saving. Since poles can usually be replaced on a piece-by-piece basis, the lifespan of the tent is usually the lifespan of the skin. Your job is to figure what percentage of its useful life is still around, and pay accordingly.

Another drawback used tents share with used cars is that you get what the original owner ordered in the way of options, which may or may not be what you wanted. Some options, such as sod flaps, are easier to retrofit than others (such as zippers or vents), so the lack of an option that you want isn't necessarily a deal-breaker. But you have to factor in the cost of the retrofit if the option is really something you want somewhere down the road.

Getting Around

When you buy a tent, you must give some thought to how you're going to transport it. The larger the tent, the more cargo space you must devote to it, which means less room for everything else you need to carry. Folks sometimes regret their purchase of a big tent when they realize that vehicles like vans, trucks, and trailers become necessities.

One item that figures prominently in the transportation equation is the tent's frame. Larger tents customarily have poles ten feet or longer that have to be accommodated somehow. One solution is to order the poles with breakdowns, which use sleeves or other hardware to assemble shorter pole segments into the longer poles that you need. This solution isn't always possible or even desirable because it generally adds to the weight and cost of the tent. In addition, it greatly increases the "fuss factor" in assembly, and gives you more pieces to lose. (And when you lose a piece of a pole, you don't have half a pole. You have no pole.) Finally, if the breakdown isn't properly designed, it can render the structure somewhat less strong than a structure without breakdowns.

When customers ask about breakdown poles because they can't fit the poles into their trucks, vans, station wagons, or what-have-you, I usually suggest that they invest in a roof rack instead. It's usually no more expensive, allows the poles to be transported full length, and can be used for other ungainly things like canoes, ladders, and the like.

Of course, you have to be careful when installing them so they don't part company with the vehicle when you're going down the freeway. So if you do decide to use roof racks, have them installed by a firm that knows what it's doing. For references, you can't beat your local hang gliding emporia. Their customers routinely put gliders worth thousands of dollars on their roof racks (often the cargo is worth more than the vehicle is), and they appreciate the value of good racks, properly installed.

But breakdown poles have some advantages of their own, not only because they are easier to transport but because they are easier to ship. Often, the savings from shipping will pay for the cost of the breakdowns.

Practice, practice, practice

When my father worked at the Central Intelligence Agency, he saw a sign in some office at their headquarters in McLean, Virginia. It said, "Adventure is the result of poor planning." He never forgot that message.

Whether your tent is bought new or used, practice setting it up at home, with good weather and lots of time at your disposal. That way, you'll be given the chance to get acquainted with your new toy and see how it all goes together. The worst time to make friends with your tent is at night, in the rain, on the opening day of the event, when you're tired and wet and out of patience. Believe me, a few practice runs in ideal conditions will pay for themselves many times over.

21

2. How to make your tent poles look better and last longer

If you buy a tent from most of the established tentmakers, the tent poles are usually delivered unfinished. Several reasons are given for this. The tentmaker might be trying to reduce his manufacturing costs and, subsequently, the price of the tent. Or maybe the factory wanted to leave the choice of finish up to you, based on your particular requirements of authenticity vs. practicality. (And it's true that changing a finish that's already on the pole usually involves removing the previous finish entirely, which is quite a chore.) Any of these reasons is quite valid.

But you should finish them yourself, and as soon as possible. Here's why.

When the tree is cut down, it has a lot of water in it (up to 80% of its weight, I'm told). As the wood is exposed to air, it gradually loses most of its moisture content and stabilizes at roughly the ambient humidity of the air. This process can either occur naturally, as part of the wood's "seasoning" process, or it can be accelerated by baking the wood in huge kilns. In the process of seasoning, some change occurs in the wood's dimensions. That's why woodworkers and lumber mills usually like to use well-seasoned wood; it's more likely to remain at the same dimensions they cut and milled it to.

We want our poles to stay in the shape we received them in, too. The trouble is that if the wood is again exposed to sudden, drastic changes in moisture, it will absorb that water unevenly, resulting in warping and bending. One side of the pole swells, but the other side doesn't, so the pole warps. A pole that's bent much more than one diameter out of column (that is, the deflection in the pole's dimension from a straight line is greater than the pole's diameter), its ability to carry a load is severely diminished. Gradually, the moisture diffuses itself so that it's more or less equal throughout the wood, but that's no guarantee that the wood will revert to its former shape.

The key words in the previous paragraph are "sudden" and "drastic." We don't want to seal the wood completely, since that would promote wood rot. What we want to do is slow down the absorption of moisture into the wood, so the wood won't absorb water faster than it can evenly distribute. And that's where pole finishes come in.

In this chapter, I'm deliberately ignoring finishes, like lacquer, which are used not to retard moisture but to increase the surface hardness and improve the looks of the wood. They aren't suitable for the job we have in mind, which is to provide a water-resistant (but slightly permeable) membrane to reduce water absorption.

We don't know for sure what was used in medieval times for this purpose. It is quite possible that nothing was used. Of all the furniture and woodwork which has survived, very little shows much evidence of finishing. Since wood was pretty prevalent in most of the areas that large pavilion-style tents were found in, it would have made more sense logistically to cut poles on the spot rather than transport them around. If poles were cut on-site, the wood would have been so green that finishing it wouldn't have accomplished anything.

If a period tentmaker had wanted to finish his tent poles anyway, there were a few finishing methods that were known to have been in use then. He could have used animal fat, linseed oil, or beeswax. Animal fat has the nasty habit of going rancid after a while, which means that you probably won't want to use that method for your own poles.

Beeswax is applied by melting it and thinning it with mineral spirits, and then applying it to the finish with a brush or rag. The mineral spirits make the wax much easier to apply. Several coats are necessary, with some rubbing to cure the finish.

Linseed oil is used much the same way. You need boiled linseed oil, by the way, not raw linseed oil. Raw linseed takes forever and a day to cure. The boiled variety (which isn't really boiled -- at least not nowadays -- but treated with metallic driers to make it cure faster) is the stuff used in making paints and finishes because it reacts with the oxygen in the air to form a relatively hard surface, with heat as a by-product. (Enough heat is generated, by the way, to ignite any oil-soaked rags, so you don't want to leave these lying around in your garage. Instead, keep those rags immersed in water until the oil hardens.)

Diluting the oil with mineral spirits makes it easier to apply, but really doesn't affect penetration much. As you apply the oil, you'll notice that some parts of the wood suck up the oil faster than other parts, resulting in dry spots. Just keep applying the oil until these spots disappear, then wipe off the excess. After letting the finish dry overnight, sand it down to eliminate the roughness in the finish and apply another coat of oil. Repeat at least another coat or two, letting the finish dry overnight and sanding between coats.

Both of the above treatments don't really result in a hard finish, so they aren't generally used in any application where you want some resistance to scratches. About the only use I've heard of for beeswax finishes nowadays is in the making of woodworking benches, where you want any scratches to be on the workbench, not the work. They have the additional drawback of requiring replenishment on a regular basis (usually yearly).

Another natural oil is tung oil, but I have no information on whether this was used in period, at least in Europe. It dries harder than linseed oil, but takes longer to cure and requires more coats. If you go this route, please be advised that most of the "tung oil finishes" or "tung oil varnishes" you find in the stores, like Formby's, are mostly varnish, not tung oil.

Being a lazy person at heart, I use modern varnishes rather than period finishes. They're cheaper and easier to apply, and last longer. If you use "satin" or "semi-gloss" finishes, they won't look too tacky. To use them, just follow the instructions on the can or bottle. Be sure to finish the top and bottom of each pole, because it's the ends that are most likely to wick up moisture. Wood is comprised of bundles of long cellulose tubes, and the ends of the pole are where the ends of those tubes are exposed. (If you go to an outdoor lumberyard, you may notice that somebody's painted the ends of all those two-by-fours. That's to seal the ends of the tubes and keep moisture from getting in.)

Most of the varnishes are about the same, dollar for dollar, but there's one kind that's formulated especially for stuff that's out in the open and exposed to the elements all the time. It's called "spar varnish" and it's used by the boating trade to coat – well, spars. And masts. And other exposed woodwork. It has a dollop more of the UV inhibitors that outdoor use requires. Another difference is that it doesn't dry as hard as your garden-variety varnishes. That is to say, it's not at all tacky, but it retains a little resilience, much like a vinyl coating. For tent poles, this is a good thing, because a finish that stays supple isn't as likely to crack when we bang two poles together (which happens to the best of us when we're loading up).

Due to increasing concern about paint solvents and the environment, we're starting to see a lot of water-based varnishes. Once cured, they're said to be as durable and water-resistant as the spirits-based formulations. I haven't found that to be the case so far, but they are getting better all the time, and are close to the performance of the spirit-based varnishes at this point.

One final piece of advice is: buy the best stuff you can find. The cheaper varnishes cost less because they have less of the stuff it takes to do the job, and more solvent. And in the case of the water-based varnishes, you're paying the big manufacturers more because they've invested more bucks in the research and development that it takes to put their new product on the market, and you're presumably getting the fruits of those labors. Economizing here really doesn't make sense. If a more expensive varnish lasts a few seasons longer and protects better, it's a bargain even at the higher price.

One arguably period form of paint is milk paint, which has been around, in one form or another, since the days of the Pharoahs. We don't know exactly how this was compounded in medieval Europe, or how extensively it was used, but the modern formulations available from specialty woodworking suppliers seem to be close in appearance to the paint on surviving medieval articles. It's relatively trouble-free to mix and apply, but it does tend to "spot" on contact with water and therefore requires an additional moisture barrier such as the aforementioned oils and varnishes.

How to paint the poles, bottoms and all

Figure 11. Using nails to support the poles

The trick to getting the paint (or varnish, or what have you) on the entire length of the pole, and the bottom as well, is to drive two nails into the bottom of the pole. When the poles are laid on a pair of sawhorses, the nails support the bottoms of the poles, and the spikes support the tops, so none of the wood is actually touching the sawhorses.

Paint the top of the pole and, grabbing either the spike or the nails, turn the pole over. Because you used two nails per pole, the pole won't want to roll, and the pole will stay in whatever orientation you have it. When the pole is dry, pull out the nails and fill the holes with putty or candle wax or whatever else you have lying around that will seal the holes.

If you're painting poles of varying lengths, there are a couple of tricks you can use, as the following illustration suggests:

Figure 12. Other Ways to Support Pole Ends.

These are the same four poles that you saw in the last illustration. The two long poles in the rear have spikes, which are used to support the ends of the poles on the sawhorse. The one in front also has a spike, but it's a lot shorter than the others, so I've supported the spike end with a piece of cheap PVC pipe clamped to the sawhorse. The spike goes into the PVC, which is clamped at a suitable distance to support the pole.

The last pole, just behind the short one in front, has a sleeve attached to it. I've fashioned an extension out of a scrap piece of pole and inserted it into the sleeve, so it too can be supported at both ends by the sawhorses.

3. Ropes, Stakes, and Hammers

Later in this chapter, we'll talk about using ropes and stakes to keep your tent attached to terra firma in even the most extreme conditions. But first, we'll discuss the ropes and stakes themselves. It's obvious that your connection is only as good as the stake and rope itself. Here's how to get the most of what you have.

Knowing the ropes

When you're selecting rope for your tent, you have to decide up front whether you're going to go for a natural fiber rope (like cotton, manila, hemp or sisal) or artificial-fiber (like polyester, polypropylene, or Nylon). The choice will be aesthetics and authenticity versus stability and durability.

If you're going for authenticity, the most historically accurate cordage is probably hemp. It also handles very well, is fairly smooth, and holds knots well. Unfortunately, it's also rather hard to come by, at least in the United States of America, since laws regulating the growing of marijuana also apply to growing hemp. However, it can be imported, and there are suppliers in eastern Europe whose wares can be had.

Hemp can be notoriously variable in quality, ranging from nearly as soft as cotton rope to nearly as stiff and fibrous as manila, but most of the stuff we see nowadays runs to the softer side. It also tends to be a bit more variable in thickness, so it's wise to test if your rope can go through the slider easily.

A slider is a little gadget, usually consisting of a piece of wood with two holes in it, used for tightening and loosening guy ropes. I recommend that you use them with hemp rope, rather than tying sliding knots such as the tautline hitch (which I'll describe anon). The reason is that when hemp rope gets wet, it contracts and swells. (I've heard that in some circumstances, the rope contracts enough to tear the stakes right out of the ground after a good soaking rain, although that phenomenon may have as much to do with soggy ground and inadequate stakes as the contraction of the rope.) This means that you have to pay more attention to hemp ropes than other kinds, loosening them when the weather gets damp and tightening up when it dries out again. It also means that, when the rope starts to swell, it's nearly impossible for a sliding knot to slide, so some sort of sliders are very helpful here.

Here's a diagram of the kind of slider I use for my tents:

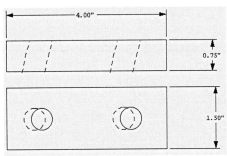

Figure 13. A Rope Slide

The length is really not critical; the greater the length, the more leverage you can put on them but the more slack they put into the rope when released. Our sliders are made from 1" x 2" (which is actually 1-1/2" by ¾") red oak, available at most large lumber centers. Don't use plywood or softwood. The holes are 1/8" larger than the diameter of your rope. Note that the holes are drilled at an angle.

The slider should be threaded so that it's canted upward when the main part of the rope is tight but the rest of it (the part with the knot) is slack. This increases the "bite" on the rope when the slider is tightened. Another way to increase the grip in the rope is to make sure that the final length of the rope is threaded through the top of the slider, as shown at right, instead of from the bottom. Be sure to "chamfer" or bevel the edges of the hole so they won't eat into the rope.

Figure 14. Threaded Rope Slide

If you want an authentic rope but don't want hemp, your choice is pretty much a toss-up between manila and sisal. Both are easily obtainable just about everywhere. Their strengths are quite similar (manila is about 20% stronger) and both hold knots reasonably well. They do stretch under load, particularly when damp. And if stored wet, both will rot.

I've noticed that most of the manila rope I've come across has been lightly oiled, and I suspect that if it weren't, it would probably demonstrate the same sort of swelling and contracting that hemp does. If you use this sort of rope, beware: when the rope is left in contact with the canvas during storage, some of that oil will eventually migrate onto the fabric, resulting in unsightly blotches. So make sure to store the ropes in a bag of their own.

One drawback of manila or ropes is that sliding knots (used to regulate the length and tension of the ropes) don't hold very well. So, again, you'll want to use some sort of slider.

Bringing up the rear of the natural-rope procession is cotton. Besides sharing all the disadvantages of the other ropes (stretch and susceptibility to rot), cotton also holds knots so tenaciously that once tied, the knot is very difficult to untie. With sliding knots, the difficulty isn't that they'll come loose, but that they won't slide easily. Cotton is also weaker. Even a reinforced-core cotton braided rope is only half the strength of a manila cord with the same diameter. And cotton wouldn't have been a choice in period, since the process of removing the seeds was so labor-intensive that cotton was reserved for cloth-making (and precious little of that, compared with the more commonly available fibers like flax, hemp, and wool).

Artificial-fiber ropes are your choice if stability and longevity are your primary concerns. Of the various fibers available, only polyester (which Dupont markets under the trade name of Dacron) is a practical fiber. It holds knots well (although the knots can be undone if necessary) and it is relatively impervious to moisture, sunlight, or rot. A #6 "diamond braid" (about 3/16" or 4.5 mm in diameter) is as heavy as you need to go for most guy ropes; it has twice the tensile strength of a manila rope when new, and keeps its strength far longer than manila or sisal. For lines that bear higher loads, such as wind lines, #8 (one quarter-inch or 6 mm) is plenty.

Nylon is a (distant) second choice to polyester. It too is very strong, but it is more susceptible to sunlight damage and its tension is strongly affected by temperature. It expands when cold, decreasing tension, and it contracts when warm, increasing tension.

Polypropylene is pretty horrible as a rope, since it is slippery, doesn't hold knots well, is fairly weak, and looks extremely tacky in its more fluorescent manifestations (although you can buy it in a color that closely approximates hemp). About the only good thing I can say for it is that it floats ... not an important consideration for tents. Let us speak no more of this rope.

The "tautline" hitch is a good slip knot that works well with most synthetic rope, and it's not too difficult to tie. Figure 15, on the next page, shows how to do it.

With all ropes, it's important to check them once in a while for integrity. Check for fraying, broken fibers, and funny smells. Ensure that the knots are staying knotted. The most common points of wear are at the points where it attaches to a stake or to the tent, or anyplace where it's forced around a small radius. Remember that any place where the rope has a knot, it has a weak point. And if the rope has experienced strain, that weak

29

point remains, to some extent, even if the knot is later untied. (Don't be unduly alarmed about this. The rope will likely still have enough strength to be used as a guy rope. I'm mentioning

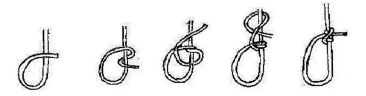

Figure 15. How to Tie a Tautline Hitch

this to emphasize that no rope is immortal, and that the rope that your buddy borrowed to pull his truck out of the mud may not be as strong as it used to be.)

How strong is that rope?

Here's a table of comparative tensile strengths for most of the types of rope we've been discussing.

Comparative Strengths of Ropes			
Composition	Thickness	Tensile Strength (Lbs)	Tensile Strength (Kg)
Reinforced-core cotton	1/8" (3 mm)	130	59
Reinforced-core cotton	3/16" (4.75 mm)	180	82
Reinforced-core cotton	1/4" (6 mm)	250	114
Polyester or nylon awning braid	1/8" (3 mm)	450	205
Polyester or nylon awning braid	3/16" (4.75 mm)	750	341
Polyester or nylon awning braid	1/4" (6mm)	1100	500
Manila	1/4" (6 mm)	540	245
Manila	5/16" (8 mm)	843	375
Manila	3/8" (9.5 mm)	1220	555
Sisal	1/4" (6 mm)	480	218
Sisal	5/16" (8 mm)	800	364
Sisal	3/8" (9.5 mm)	108	491
Hemp	1/4" (6 mm)	404	187
Hemp	5/16" (8 mm)	803	365
Hemp	3/8" (9.5 mm)	1540	700

Bear in mind that the figures for the natural fibers can be considered approximate (nobody tells the plants what the desired specifications are as they are growing, so they don't know), and that "working" strengths are approximately 10% of the actual tensile strength.

Also remember that these are for ropes in new condition, and that rope weakens with age. Hemp rope, in particular, has a reputation for rotting from the inside out (because that's the part that stays wet the longest), so even a visual inspection may not reveal a weakened rope.

How to Make Your Ropes Last Longer

If you use tent stakes made of square stock, you may have noticed that the edges of the stake tend to chew up ropes, causing them to wear out prematurely. In fact, except for mildew and rot, this is the major cause of premature failure of tent ropes.

There are two fixes for this problem. The first involves sliding a piece of hose (like discarded garden hose) onto the shaft of the stake, and adjusting the position of the hose segment so that it acts as a cushion for the rope. This works well, but unless you're using black hose, it will show up fairly conspicuously, which may detract somewhat from the look of your campsite. And since you're transferring the wear point from the stake to the hose, you may have to replace the segments periodically.

The second method, which I prefer, is to thread the rope through a 1" (25 mm) plated-steel ring. You can buy these rings at your hardware store or through Tandy Leather (Tandy sells

them for $2.50 for a packet of ten, and your hardware store probably sells them for whatever they can get for them). Be sure to get the "solid" types, which are welded shut. Now the stake makes contact with the ring instead of the rope, and the rope itself will wrap itself around the rounded radius of the ring rather than the edge of the

Figure 16. Ring on a rope

stake. And because the ring is round, each time you set up the ring will present a different contact point with the stake, which keeps the ring from developing a wear spot against the stake.

You could also grind sharp edges off the stake at the point where the rope makes contact with it, but unless that area was smoothed, the rope will still experience wear from the roughened surface of the stake. A chrome-plated ring, on the other hand, will retain its smoothness for a long time, and when the plating eventually gets beat-up, you can always replace the ring.

One of the most important components of any roping system are flags of some sort. These can be as simple as strips of white cloth tied to the rope at intervals, or as elaborate as a separate strip of dagged material pinned to it. They are important because they help prevent injuries to pedestrians and to the tent itself. It's amazing how ropes tend to vanish from sight once it gets dark, and ropes which were easy to see in daylight become invisible at night. The flags should be white or yellow, because other colors, even bright red or orange, don't stand out in the dark.

Stakes

The very best tent stakes I've seen are the kind that I've sold with my tents (for approximately the same reason that Bentleys come with leather seat covers and not vinyl). These pegs are made of 1/2" square steel stock, with one end curved to a radius of about an inch (as shown in figure 15, above), to form a hook for the tent ropes; the other end is forged (not filed or ground) to a point. These puppies are heavy, but very strong. (Usually, when I drive them in and they hit a rock, the rock loses.) But their best feature is that when it's time to take them out, you simply feed another stake (or similar object) through the curve and rotate the stake a quarter-turn. The square hole that the stake made when it went in becomes a round hole, and we all know about square pegs (or stakes) and round holes. A gentle tug, and these stakes seem to fly out of the hole.

We usually provide the stakes in two lengths. For guy ropes that take a lot of strain, we use 16" stakes, which are actually made of stock that's 19" long before the end is bent into a hook. For ropes that take very little load, and for staking down the bottoms of the tent sidewalls, we provide 12" stakes (which start out life as 15" pieces). For most of the camping we do, that's overkill, but now and then you come across very loose or sandy soil, and every inch counts. If the soil is very loose and conditions are windy, even these lengths might not be enough, and you'll need to resort to the tactics discussed later in this chapter. But in most situations, the ground will be fine for that length of stake. The only time that long stakes are a drawback is when the ground is very hard, but I can get all the holding power I need simply by driving the stake in nearly parallel to the ground, into the top three inches where the soil is looser.

Why 1/2" stock? Well, we tried 3/8" and it just wasn't strong enough. We've also thought about providing them in 8" lengths, but the cost probably would have been the same as the longer stakes and they wouldn't have been as versatile.

You can make an excellent stake for lighter duty, like staking down the bottom of sidewalls, using three things:

- A 12" nail, also called a "wire spike." The spike will be 3/8" in diameter. These nails are available in just about any of the larger hardware stores. (If you're buying a lot of these and you live in logging county, don't be surprised if they write down your license number as you drive off; these nails are also used by "tree spikers" to sabotage the saw blades in sawmills. In fact, you might want to keep this book handy if pointed questions are asked.)
- A washer that fits closely onto the spike. 3/8" washers will do but are a little loose. A better fit might be a 5/16" washer, which may actually have a 3/8" hole, but be sure to test the washer on the spike before you buy.
- A 1" length of thick "high pressure" hose, available from auto parts stores if your hardware store doesn't have it. Again, 3/8" will work, but if you can get one in a slightly smaller inner diameter, it will hold better. (I use 5/16" hose.) The wall thickness should be about 1/4", which means that the tube's inner diameter should be about 1/2" less than the outer diameter.

To assemble the stake, you put the washer onto the nail and slide it up toward the head. Then you put the tubing onto the nail and slide it up toward the head so that it will retain the washer. (If you have a welding rig, you can also weld the washers to the nail instead of using tubing.)

Pretty simple, huh? And this tent stake, which will cost you maybe sixty cents, will last for a very long time. You might have to replace the tubing every second year or so, and straighten it if you hit some incredibly hard stone underneath the surface, but that's about it for maintenance.

You can make smaller versions of the above stakes, using appropriately scaled-down components, to help hold rugs and mats in place in your encampment.

One drawback with all the kinds of stakes mentioned above is that they'll rust. So you'll want to have separate bags or boxes to store them in. If you're sewing-impaired, you can make a fairly good bag by taking a leg from that old pair of blue jeans and sealing one end with a hand-sewn seam, a knot, or whatever. Or check with your bank to see if they're retiring any coin sacks.

Another option is to look in thrift stores for those canvas carry-on bags (the kind with a zippered top and a shoulder strap). I usually can find them for about two or three dollars apiece. If they're the right length, they'll work fine.

How to set tent stakes

It amazes me that I actually have to write a paragraph or two on this, but I've seen so many campers – even experienced campers – set their stakes ineffectively that I figured that the advice was necessary. There are three things that you have to do to set the stake effectively.

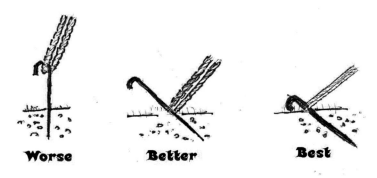

Figure 17. Setting tent stakes properly

- **Set the stake out far enough.** You need to give the rope enough length to counteract the leverage on the top of the pole that it connects to. My usual rule of thumb on this is that a minimum distance should be two-thirds of the length of the pole itself. More cautious people recommend at least one pole length out, and I would have no problem recommending that, if it weren't for the fact that the farther out the stake, the more of a tripping hazard the rope presents. If you do this, make doubly sure that the ropes are easy to spot (by flagging them well) or detour around (by putting buckets, benches, or other objects underneath the rope that people will see and avoid.) Certainly, if it's windy, increase that footprint!
- **Set the stake at an angle that is at least 90° to the rope, not to the ground.** *Never* make this angle less than 90°, because it makes the stake much, much easier to pull out of the ground. In fact, a little more is better, because it prevents the rope from slipping up the stake if it proves impossible to drive the stake completely into the ground. And you want the rope to be right next to the ground itself; otherwise, exposed length of the stake acts as a lever to help pull the stake out of the ground.

- **Use all of the stake's length if you can.** If the ground is very hard, or if there's a good root network in the sod, it's possible to lay the stake at an angle of only 15° and still have enough holding power.

If it's windy, there are even more things you can do to keep yourself connected to terra firma.

- Use longer stakes. Many people have pieces of re-bar, 18" or longer. My usual preference is to drive a surveyor's stake or a piece of 1" x 2" furring lumber (at least a foot long or so and pointed at one end) into the ground, with the wide side facing the tent, and then drive in the tent stake immediately

Figure 18. Using a stake widener

behind it (that is, against the side of the slat that isn't facing the tent), so that the tent ropes pull the stake tight against the slat. This works because it's not so much the depth of the stake that counts, but the area of stake that presents itself to the dirt. The slat effectively triples the width of the stake. Since it's biodegradable, it can be left in the ground when you pull up stakes, as long as you drive the exposed part completely into the ground, so it doesn't interfere with any mowing machine that comes along later.

- Use more stakes. Tie additional lengths of rope to each of the rope pins (or loops, or spikes, or however your ropes fasten to your tent) and run them out to their own stakes. Don't get them too close to the other stakes. Or, if you don't have more rope, you can use two stakes per rope, driving them at angles to each other (but still canted outward).

- Increase your footprint. Extend the ropes beyond their usual distance from the tent to reduce the leverage that the pole has on the ropes. The only trouble with this method, as I said earlier, is that it creates more of a tripping hazard, so make sure the ropes are well flagged.

- Use wind lines. These are special ropes that are attached to the center-pole spikes after the spikes go though the canopy, but before the center poles are raised. They extend out from the tent and then are staked down as far away from the tent as practicable. The idea is to stabilize the tops of the center poles and thereby prevent sway. Obviously, this method isn't something you can easily employ once the tent is erected, particularly if you have to partially dismantle the tent in a freshening storm. So you need to keep track of the weather forecasts, and have the ropes in place when you set up if it looks like it's going to be windy.

Most of the manufacturers of larger tents use wind lines routinely. On the other hand, all but the largest pavilions I've made have been through the horror-story windstorms you've heard about (the famous "Estrella hurricane" of many years back, the Twenty Five Year Celebration, and innumerable foul-weather Pennsics and tourneys) without needing wind lines at all. My library of pavilion representations shows a few of the very largest tents using wind lines, which may have been because they were also used for setting up the tents as well. (Of course, other artists may simply have neglected to draw them because they seemed superfluous to the scene at hand.)

Hammers

Once upon a time, we considered including a hammer with each tent so we could advertise that you get "everything you need to set up your camp ... including the hammer!" But after surveying people's preferences, we concluded that it would be impossible to satisfy everybody's requirements.

Brawny people want a heavy hammer (at least three pounds) to deliver the maximum of persuasion to the stake with a minimum of swings. Those with weaker wrists or less upper body strength might find such a hammer hard to control, and have better luck delivering more blows with a lighter hammer (one to two pounds). Hammer weight, by the way, is defined by the weight of the head, not the weight of the entire hammer including the handle.

Where possible, get a hammer with a longer handle and use the entire handle's length.

With stake pounding comes, inevitably, stake pulling. The curved-head stakes that I've described above don't need a puller, but the nail-type stakes do. Again, there are choices. Some folks (like myself) like to carry a separate crowbar of a design that lets them pull stakes without having to crawl around on the ground. Others want to save the weight, and instead use a claw hammer, which provides both stake-pounding and stake-pulling functions in one tool. The framing hammers with the long, straight claws and the heavier heads work well for this.

If you're driving stakes into very hard ground and have water to spare, try soaking the ground with water first to soften it up. If the weather is very dry, you may find that you have to soak the ground again to pull the stakes up.

If you're the type that gets to the site late and find yourself setting up large tents in the middle of the night, you will make many friends if you use a "dead blow" hammer. This tool looks a lot like a rubber mallet, but its rubber-covered head is actually made of metal, hollow, and partially filled with lead shot. As the hammer strikes the stake, the lead shot delivers the oomph a fraction of a second after the hammer makes contact with the stake, resulting in near-silent operation rather than a midnight rendition of the *Anvil Chorus*.

Hammers last a long time, unless their handles get chewed up. This condition occurs when you repeatedly miss the stake and the handle takes the brunt of the blow. After a while, the handle becomes weak enough to make the hammer unsafe, and has to be replaced. To prolong the life of my hammers, I wrap a piece of rubber around the handle just below the head to provide a few layers of rubber cushion for that occasional missed blow. Discarded bicycle tires work wonderfully for that, and your local bike shop will probably give you all you need for free.

4. How to Wash Your Tent

Well, you're back from whatever dirty, dusty event you've most recently attended. Your tent, once white as snow, now bears soil samples from every place it's been pitched. And those mud tracks across the roof are particularly embarrassing. So it's time to wash the tent.

An afternoon of soap, water, and elbow grease can make your tent look years younger, and if done correctly, it can add years of life to it. This is because when dirt gets into the weave of the cloth, the gritty particles actually wear into the threads, chafing them and weakening them, resulting in premature failure of the cloth.

We'll assume that your tent is a canvas tent from one of the major tentmakers, and that the canvas has had some treatment for water-repellency, and possibly for fire-retardance and mildew resistance as well. Most of what follows applies to other fabric as well, although you might want to test the methods on some inconspicuous part of the tent, particularly if you think that the colorfastness of your tent might be in doubt.

The trick to washing canvas is to float the dirt and debris away from the fabric instead of grinding it into the fabric's weave. The best procedure is to apply a light spray to wet the fabric, follow this wetting with a soap application to encapsulate all the tiny bits of dirt and float them off the cloth, and finish the job with a thorough rinse at somewhat higher water pressure to eliminate all traces of the soap solution. Allow the newly cleaned tent to dry completely, and voila! a clean tent.

Or a cleaner tent, anyway. Don't expect miracles, particularly with some of the finer varieties of dirt or with oil-based stains. At one An Tir/West War in southern Oregon, the site became blanketed with a fine red dust that would have been useful for making pigments. It got into everything and gave all the white tents on site a distinct terra-cotta hue. Dust this fine is very difficult to remove with an ordinary soap-and-water treatment, and it may be helpful to first vacuum – not brush – as much dust as you can off the fabric before commencing with the washing operation.

To wash your tent, you need to have a warm, rainless period of sufficient duration to allow the tent to dry completely. To ascertain the weather patterns, ancient wisdom counsels that you slaughter a small rodent or bird and study the entrails carefully for clues to the coming weather, but some folks may prefer to watch the weather report on the evening news instead. *

Now for tools. My general rule for soap is not to use anything that I wouldn't mind having my hands in for a while. Mild detergents intended for hand-washing dishes are ideal. Anything stronger might damage the various treatments that the cloth was given at the mill.

The best brush is one with soft bristles and a long handle. They are intended for washing cars without damaging the paint; you find these in the automotive section of the larger discount stores. For what it's worth, my current brush is called the Hoppy Brush and was bought at my local Kmart for about twenty dollars. It has a telescoping handle and can be connected to a garden hose, although that makes the brush very ungainly to use, and the small size of the built-in nozzle constricts the water flow to a puny trickle. I just use the brush for soaping and scrubbing, and the hose with the standard spray nozzle for wetting and rinsing. The bristles are stiff enough to scrub the cloth, but not so stiff that they end up grinding the dirt into the fabric.

Figure 19. Hanging the Tent Sides

Anyway, you've got your tools and your bright sunny day. It's time to roll up your sleeves and get to work. If the sections you're washing are flat ones, like the tent sides, you can lay them out on the lawn and scrub them there, rinse them off, and then hang them vertically to dry. Since I had about fifteen feet of garage wall handy, I nailed up some scrap conduit so I could leave the sides hanging for as long as it took to dry (see Figure 19). If you haven't such a handy expanse of wall, or a really strong clothesline, you can of course set the tent up in the usual way and hang the sides off the tent. But

_____

* Note to animal rights advocates: This is a *JOKE*. The author does not actually advocate your killing of said animals to perform this ritual, and suggest it only if your cat – who is probably not an animal rights advocate, except where cats are concerned – has already donated a small rodent or bird to the cause.)

try to keep the sides (including the sod flaps) away from contact with the ground until they dry.

Figure 20: A retainer for the center pole's upper segment

I've found that the most efficient way to clean the roof sections is to set it up close to the ground, using shortened center poles. If you're washing a round tent with a rigid ring, it's possible to set the tent up using a short version of your center-pole, or the upper half of a breakdown center pole. To avoid having to guy the tent, drive two pieces of angle iron into the ground for about a third of its length, forming a socket into which you can insert the center pole (see Figure 20).

The tent goes onto the top of the pole, and the bottom of the roof is tensioned by the ring or spokes or whatever. If your tent does not have such a structure, you can stake out the roof, whatever its shape, in the usual way, using shortened ropes. The advantage of using a shorter center pole is that the canvas is more easily available for cleaning, being at eye level rather than way over your head. (See Figure 21.) The principal disadvantage is that you can't use the canopy as a place to hang the sidewalls up to dry, as you could if the tent were set up in the conventional way.

Figure 21: The roof at eye level for cleaning

Scrub the cloth gently. I use a side-to-side motion of the brush to maximize the number of bristles in action at each pass, as shown in Figure 22. It seems to do a better job than moving the bristles up and down. Remember that using excessive pressure or a stiffer brush can result in the dirt being ground deeper into the cloth, rather than being

40

floated away from it.

When you're finished with the soap phase of your project, rinse the tent well. Then rinse it again. After you're done with that, rinse it again. And have I told you to rinse it really well? You really must rinse all traces of the soap away, because soap, moisture, and sunlight form a

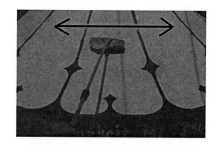

Figure 22. Scrubbing the tent

deadly combination for fabric. Of these three things, the only one you can control is the amount of soap, so for the sake of your tent's lifespan, that amount should be zero.

Be sure to let the tent pieces dry thoroughly before putting them away. Remember that with all this washing and rinsing and rinsing and rinsing, your tent is a lot wetter than it is likely to get even from a downpour. All-cotton tents may require days of warm weather to dry thoroughly enough to prevent mildew infestation. If you're drying the tent indoors, fans help greatly to move the air around and speed up the drying process.

5. Tent Repairs Simplified

A few years ago, there appeared a very funny book by Dereck Williamson called *The Complete Book of Pitfalls – A Homeowner's Guide to Repairs, Maintenance, and Repairing the Maintenance.* The title neatly acknowledges the fact that many repair jobs end up doing more damage than they fix. The purpose of this article is to help you avoid that particular pitfall, and to help you get your tent back into service with a minimum of travail.

The Fabric

For an in-the-field repair, you can usually rely on good old duct tape. It will look ugly, but will keep your tent dry inside. If the rip is extensive, try using a series of longer strips perpendicular to the rip to bring the edges of the tear back together, and then seal the rip itself with a single strip of tape parallel to the rip. Otherwise, a single strip of tape might not be strong enough to keep the edges of the tear from separating again under load. Don't leave the tape on any longer than necessary, because that glue can be hell to clean off.

Your first task, when you get your tent back home, is to determine whether a permanent repair is feasible in the first place. No fabric is immortal, and there comes a time when the cloth becomes so weakened that repairs are simply not worth the trouble. After all, most repairs involve sewing, and no repair will be stronger than the material that holds the stitches. And when you strengthen an area with patches, glue, or the like, the tension simply gets transferred to an adjacent area which may not be long from failure for the same reason that the first area failed. I have often refused to do repairs on sails and tents, lucrative though they might have been, because there was simply not enough strength left in the remaining cloth to have made the repair worthwhile. Putting good thread into bad cloth makes no sense, because the repair will inevitably fail. It's the old principle about the chain being only as strong as ... um ... now how does that go?

Don't be afraid to try to extend the rip a little. If it's very easy to do, you can be sure that the cloth is not long for this world, and that any repair is not likely to hold up for long. You'll have to consider the age of the tent, the conditions it has faced (and is likely to face in the future) and how much future unreliability you are willing to put up with. Sometimes it's better to replace, not repair.

But some repairs do make sense. In fact, they almost always make sense if the defect is due to anything but cloth failure. Cloth will get punctured from a high point-load, improperly seated grommets may fail, and occasionally the tent is subjected to freak forces which it was never designed for in the first place, and which it will likely never encounter again. A good repair here should greatly extend the life of the tent and, if properly done, will be as strong as it was before.

A rip caused by point-loading (like when an errant tent pole poked through it) is best fixed by sewing a little patch of the same material onto it. Fold over each side of the patch to keep it from fraying, and sew it to the outside surface of the damaged

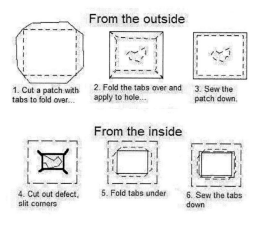

From the outside

1. Cut a patch with tabs to fold over...

2. Fold the tabs over and apply to hole...

3. Sew the patch down.

From the inside

4. Cut out defect, slit corners

5. Fold tabs under

6. Sew the tabs down

Figure 23. How to prepare and sew a patch

area. If you want to keep the damaged area itself from fraying, make the patch large enough that you can cut away the damaged area and leave enough of the tent fabric to be folded under and then sewn to the patch. (See Figure 23, above.)

The only trouble with this sort of patch is that you usually have to seal the upper seam of the patch on the outside. Otherwise, top of the patch forms a lip that can collect water that can leak through the seam. This sealing can be done with a product designed for this very purpose and available at K marts and sporting good stores, or with any cement that dries hard and flexible. You could also treat it with a moisture-repellent spray like Scotch-Gard or Camp-Dry, but this may require periodic re-treatment.

Another good way to patch a tear is by gluing on a patch. When you use glue, the fabric won't fray and the repair won't leak. But you must use a glue which adheres to the tent reliably under all the conditions (heat, cold, moisture, flexion, etc.) that the tent is likely to endure.

The best glue I've found is Barge's Cement, made by the Quabaug Corporation of North Brookfield, Masssachusetts. Many hardware stores carry it, and it's worth taking the trouble to find it. (No, I don't own stock in the corporation; I just like the product. We always have it in our tool box, right next to the duct tape.) It works like most contact cements, where you apply a film of it to each surface to be joined, let the film dry, and bring the surfaces together. Barge's Cement outshines the other contact cements in its ability to stay flexible after it has cured in just about any conceivable conditions you tent is likely to encounter, and over long periods of time. I've found that the strength of the joint can be greatly increased if, after you've joined the surfaces together, you beat on the joint with a mallet to fuse the films together. (Be sure to have a solid backing on the other side of the cloth, of course.) Before applying the cement to the fabric, it helps to clean the spot and the patch with denatured alcohol to remove any previous fabric treatment and the accumulated grunge of the outdoors.

If either sewing a patch on or gluing it on doesn't appeal to you, there's a third way using a product called *HeatnBond Ultrahold* from Therm O Web. I got some at my local Hancock's Fabrics, but it should be available from other fabric shops as well. It's an iron-on adhesive that allows you to make your own iron-on patches for your tent. First, you cut a piece of the stuff the size of the patch you want, and iron it onto the patch material. Then you remove a paper layer, lay it onto the tent fabric, and re-iron so that the patch bonds to the fabric. Voila! It seems to do a good job of sticking to the fabric, even with any treatments the fabric may have had applied to it. It should also resist the elements fairly well, since it's machine washable. It works with Sunforger, the most popular tent material, and should work with other fabrics as well, although not with canvases with an acrylic top coat. It's worth pointing out that the cleaner the fabric, the better the patch will stick.

If the failure is along a seam line, the best repair is to overlay a wide piece of fabric over the rip that's wide enough to cover the seam on one side and extend at least an inch or two beyond the rip on the other. Attach one edge of the patch to the seam itself, and trim it so it extends a few inches past the length of the rip at each end. Then sew the patch down. This allows all the fabric layers of the seam to help share the load, reducing the chance of the seam failing again at that point. Again, you must ask yourself whether the seam failed do to an unusual load or whether the cloth itself is giving up the ghost. I'm reiterating this because I've found that seam failures are far more often due to the latter cause than the former, and you may have to consider retiring the tent rather than repairing it.

When a grommet (sometimes also called an eyelet) fails, but the fabric it was mounted in remains intact, the repair usually consists of simply installing another grommet. If a grommet repeatedly fails at that location, you should replace it with a larger grommet, since the larger ones can better spread the load. If the grommet serves the purpose of restraining a knot in a rope that goes through the grommet, you may need to install a washer on the rope to keep the knot from passing through the new, larger grommet hole. If the grommet is a plain grommet, consider having a sailmaker or awning maker replace it with a rolled-rim "spur" grommet, which is designed for more rugged duty and resists separating.

When a grommet fails and takes the fabric with it, simply replacing the grommet won't do. You'll have to repair the fabric as well. I like to do this by reinforcing the area with two-inch-wide seat belt webbing and then installing a new grommet into the webbing. This webbing is thin, but amazingly strong, and is readily available (maybe even free from your local junkyard). You could also stitch in more canvas, in multiple layers. It is always better to make the patches bigger than you think they should be, since more patches fail because they are too small than because they are too big (a principle often thought to apply to other areas of life, as witnessed by the military axiom: "A lot is good, more is better, and too much is just enough.") If the grommet is located near a hem or another cloth edge, it should be set away from the edge at a distance of at least its own inside diameter, and preferably twice that (See the axiom above.)

A patch is likeliest to fail either at its edge (if the patch is located along the edge of the fabric) or at the point where it is sewn onto the fabric. In the latter case, it's the fabric, not the patch, that actually fails. This is because the cloth flexes more at the point where a great thickness (the patch) meets less thickness (the fabric), and this flexion weakens the fibers of the cloth. To prevent failure there, make sure that the edge of the patch is far enough from the grommet (or tie, or whatever dictated the patch in the first place) that the load is sufficiently reduced. When sailmakers reinforce a high-stress area, they often use multiple patches, gradually increasing the thicknesses and layers to avoid going directly from a single layer of fabric to a heavy patch. That's also how we reinforce the peaks of our canopies — from a single layer of reinforcement, to two layers, and then to two layers plus a thick 3" Nylon webbing.

I don't recommend leather as a reinforcement unless the use of period materials is really important to you. This is because leather, even more than canvas, is susceptible to rot and mildew.

45

And when dry, it tends to stiffen and crack. If you must use leather, make sure it is well tanned and treated with finishers to keep it supple and resistant to decay. I've found that pigskin tends to weather a bit better than cowhide, but tears a little easier. I haven't used leather from bison, moose, or elk, but imagine that it would work well due to its toughness and flexibility.

Because mildew can be a huge problem, it deserves a chapter of its own. That's the next chapter. But I have to remind you not to expect miracles. The more aggressive you are with mildew treatments, the more you risk damaging some of the fabric's water repellency and flame resistance. If the fabric is aging, you might be better off making sure that the mildew is killed, but leaving the stain intact. You could add even more artwork and, if people point out the stain to you, you say, "That's not a mildew stain. That's smoke coming from the castle at the siege of Heidelberg, which I've depicted here in the style of Albrecht Durer." Then you pause a beat, and add, "It *does* look a little like a mildew stain, now that you mention it." Practice your part well, and you just might pull it off.

Rust stains sometimes respond to a solution of oxalic acid (available in some hardware and drug stores), followed by washing, rinsing, and drying. Remember to rinse the fabric well, followed by more rinsing and even more rinsing. Any trace of soap remaining in the fabric will combine with UV radiation and moisture in the air to greatly weaken the cloth. This is particularly true of synthetic cloths, but applies to natural fabrics as well.

The Frame

Frame repairs usually involve replacement of the failed part, but there are a few good things to know.

A bent pole should be replaced. If it's more than two diameters out of column, it's no longer strong enough to be in your tent, because much of its strength in compression is gone. Sometimes you can strip the finish off the pole (if indeed it had any in the first place), wet the pole, and hold it in a straightening jig until it's dry. If you do this, re-finish the straightened pole immediately to keep the pole from absorbing moisture.

A broken pole can be sleeved. A good rule of thumb is to make sure the sleeve is six times longer than the diameter of the pole it repairs (that is, a pole two inch thick needs a sleeve twelve inches long, with six inches above the break and six inches below it).

In a pinch, the broken pole can also be splinted. You need three dowels or pieces of pipe, each two feet long and at least a third of the diameter of the broken pole, and some duct tape.

Space the splints equidistant to each other around the pole and hold them in place with the duct tape. You need to wrap the duct tape around the splints both immediately above and immediately below the break, and also at the tops and bottoms of the splints. This repair should hold up for the remainder of the event, but it's only a temporary fix.

If the metal extension (the part that goes into the grommet) is falling out of the top of the pole, you can glue it back in with epoxy. Or you can use a urethane glue like Gorilla Glue. These new glues expand within the space between the metal and the wood and provide an extremely durable bond. I like to clean out the hole a bit with a round wood rasp or file to remove any weak wood in the hole, figuring that the glue joint is only going to be as strong as the wood that it joins. (That's the old "A chain is only as strong..." principle at work.) Just before putting the glued spike into the hole, squirt a little water in there ... it's the water that provides the catalyst for hardening the glue. Again, make sure the top of the pole is well varnished to stabilize the wood and eliminate the shrinkage or swelling that caused the metal pin to come loose in the first place.

Parts made of rope or PVC pipe are usually not worth fixing. Just replace them. I know that PVC is wonderfully easy to repair using PVC glue and various fittings. But since the break was usually caused by the pipe getting old and weak, you again run into the problem of fastening a sound repair to a weak structure. If you enjoy repairing rather than replacing, feel free to do so; you can look forward to many hours of enjoyment because that pipe is going to keep breaking over and over again until you replace it. The problem with PVC (and EMT thinwall conduit, for that matter) is was that it was never really designed to be a structural member. It was designed to be easily bent and to hold stuff inside it, not to take any great loads.

Miscellaneous Repairs

There's not much else that can really go wrong with a tent. Zippers, if you've got them, can fail, but larger ones seldom need anything more than a new slide once every ten years or so. The smaller zippers on modern tents are more of a headache. It's such a job to have these repaired that for tents that cost less than $100-$150, it's usually better to replace the tent with a new one that has a lot more life left in it. But if the teeth are still intact and the problem is that the slide isn't squeezing the two sides together, sometimes the problem is that the slide itself has expanded. To fix this, simply take a pair of pliers and pinch the front and back of the slide closer together. Voila! (On big slides, you want to take two pairs of pliers – or, better still, two Vise-grip pliers – and put one on each side of the toggle. Then carefully apply pressure simultaneously to avoid distorting the slide.)

Vinyl or plastic ground cloths can be easily repaired with the kits that you get at the auto supply store to repair vinyl seat covers with.

If you have a tent that uses a rope-and-grommet arrangement for tent-stake loops, a loop repair simply consists of replacing the damaged rope segment with a good one. This repair is easy to do in the field, and requires nothing more in the way of tools than something to cut the rope with. If your design uses canvas loops, you can either sew new loops on or retrofit it with the rope-and-grommet arrangement, or simply install a very large grommet for the stake itself to pass through. Of course, you may have to add some reinforcement for the grommet. My favorite repair for ripped loops is to replace the loop with a one-inch welded steel ring, available at hardware stores or Tandy Leather. The ring is attached to the tent by a small bit of webbing sewn to the vestiges of the original loop. When the tent is set up, it's the ring that makes contact with the stake, not the webbing.

The easiest repair to make is the one you don't have to make in the first place. If you carefully follow the set-up and care instructions that came with your tent, it's quite likely that you'll never have to repair it at all. This is very easy to say, of course, and very hard to accomplish. If this were a perfect world, bad things would never happen to good people (and tents), but that's not the world we were issued, is it?

6. Combatting Mildew

Figure 24. The tent when new

A few years ago, I made the small oval tent pictured on the left. It's done duty as a storage tent and a test bed for playing around with various frame designs. I stored it in my trailer during the rainy season. To make a long story short, we had a big rainstorm, and one of the trailer's side panels warped to the point where it no longer made a weathertight seal, and water leaked in under the fabric shell. The rain came in, and the tent got wet.

When I opened the bag a month later, I found to my dismay that the sidewall panels of the tent, which were made with an untreated cotton cloth, were covered with mildew. (The canopy, made of mildew-resistant Sunforger, was still in perfect shape). I gazed bleakly at the damage and thought of the dozens of hours I'd spent in painting the design. I was not a happy camper.

My first impulse was to junk the side-walls and start over with Sunforger. But then I surveyed the available literature on mildew removal and it occurred to me that this tent would be a perfect

Figure 25. After the mildew monster visited me

lab rat for trying out the various treatments I read about. A distressing number of these treatments are described second-hand, without the author having actually tried the treatment himself. I figured there was already enough of this sort of material on the Internet, and I wanted to see what really worked and what didn't.

Besides, this gave me the opportunity to spend lots of company money on all sorts of cleaners and chemicals, and write it off as a business expense. This justification is the very heart of the expression "When life gives you lemons, make lemonade." In this case, life gave me mildew. What you get is the benefit of my misfortune, and my efforts to overcome it.

The patient

The material tested was a 6.5 oz cotton/polyester twill with no finishing process. The paint was Versatex fabric paint purchased from the Dharma Trading Company and heat-set using a commercial clothes dryer, as described on the label (and verified by a call to their customer service representative). I expect that the mildew infestation is typical of this type of cloth, as well as untreated all-cotton cloths.

Please note that mildew thrives when it finds some sort of organic food source on the fabric. It multiplies and excretes the stuff that actually causes the stain. The organic food doesn't have to be the cloth itself ... it can be organic matter on the tent such as dirt, spilled beer, or whatever. Therefore, all cloth, even synthetic cloth, is therefore susceptible to mildew damage, even when it's specifically been treated with mildew-retardant chemicals, as long as there's something for the mildew to eat. Mildew-retardant fabrics do make it a lot harder for those little buggers to survive, but I've seen mildewed Sunforger and mildewed Pyrotone.

The methodology

What follows are descriptions of the various treatments, and what I found when I used them. Please note the following caveats:

Caveat #1: I'm using a numerical rating system to help you compare the treatments. The range of these numbers is from Zero (for "didn't do squat") to Five (for "left cloth as good as new, or even better"). These numbers are not the result of careful testing, using photographs, reflective/absorptive technology, or any of the other fancy stuff that Consumers Union uses when documenting their product reviews, because I didn't have their budget. To be blunt about it, I assigned the numbers arbitrarily, on the basis of how the treatments compared. So something that rates a 3 isn't twice as effective as something that gets a 1.5 --- all it means is that it seemed to work better than something that earned a 2, and not as well as something that earned a 4. I'll bet Roger Ebert ranks movies this way, too.

Note that nobody got a 5, although some came close.

Caveat #2: I make no claim about how much any of these treatments will weaken the fabric. I suspect that some deterioration will occur, based on what I've seen bleach do to other fabrics. But I haven't tested this specifically, and I don't intend to. Instead, I'll just keep an eye on the cloth and see which sections seem to be holding up better.

Fact is, I didn't much care how badly the fabric was going to rot. As it was, it was so unsightly that I had already written it off. But if I had to choose whether to have an ugly but structurally sound cloth and a pretty but structurally damaged cloth, my choices might have been different.

I applied the treatment as described in whatever literature that accompanied the product, if it mentioned any use of it on fabric or canvas. If the product didn't mention it, I did whatever seemed right. I then gave the product about fifteen minutes to make an observable difference. If it seemed to be working, I gave it another treatment using the same method. If it didn't, I tried another treatment on the same area. However, each treatment was first tried on a new part of the cloth.

All areas were thoroughly rinsed, and rinsed, and rinsed again, using the setup I described in my column on cleaning tents. Then all the fabric was allowed to dry. Finally, I did a crude "poke test" to see if the fabric had become weakened. All the treatments survived this test, but I'll reiterate that I make no claims about how this fabric is going to age in months to come.

The results

Vinegar and Borax: This is a treatment I got off the Internet. (There's a similar formula involving lemon juice and Borax that pops up in many books on cleaning.) The attraction is that it didn't cost much. But it had practically no effect on the mildew stains. In fact, I was concerned that the vinegar might be acting as a mordant, helping to fix the discoloration into the cloth. But my wife, who does a bit of natural dying in the textiles she creates, doubted that the vinegar would have much of an effect at the temperatures I was using. **Rating: 0.5**

Shower Power from Powerworks Company: I used this on the recommendation of a fellow tentmaker, who had heard about this but hadn't actually tried it. Well, I tried it. It was a waste of money, as far as removing the stains went. To be fair, I must concede that this product was made for things like bathroom stalls, not fabric, and I suspect that it would work far better on tile and grout and stuff like that. I also suspect that most of the stuff intended to be used in shower and bath fixtures would fare about the same. No damage to painted areas. It left a strong sulfur odor, which persisted faintly even after both rinsing and subsequent treatments with other products. **Rating: 0.5**

51

Starbrite Sail & Canvas Cleaner: I got this stuff from West Marine, a marine products chain with several locations. Other marine supply companies sell a similar product. It's really a detergent, not a bleach. It foamed up real nice, but didn't make much of an impression on the mildew stains. It made the rest of the cloth nice and clean, though. I'd probably recommend it for cleaning tents if I thought that it was enough of an improvement over dish soap to justify its greater cost, but it wasn't that much better. No damage to painted areas. **Rating: 1.0**

OxiClean: This product, from Orange Glo International, also didn't specifically mention canvas, so I was left to my own ingenuity. It was recommended to me by somebody who occasionally uses it, in greatly diluted form, in her job in textile conservation and restoration. I mixed it up at the recommended strength and let the piece soak in it for twenty minutes or so. It seemed to do some, so I gave it a little longer. It did a fair job of getting the worst of the stain off, but left a distinct area where the stain was worst. Of all the products that actually seemed to get the job done, it did the least damage to the paint job. **Rating: 3.5**

West Marine Mildew And Stain Remover: Again, bought from West Marine, but they had a few other products on their shelf that seemed identical and at about the same price. Other marine supply stores have their own brands that seem to be comparable. This stuff's active ingredients are sodium hypochlorite (otherwise known as chlorine bleach) and sodium hydroxide (also known as caustic soda, liquid caustic, lye, soda lye, sodium hydrate, and other names). Like some of the other products, it didn't specifically mention canvas, but it did say it was good for boat covers, many of which are fabric, so I figured I'd give it a go. You spray it on, leave it on until the stain goes away, and rinse. No scrubbing required. It worked very well on the tent. There were some areas that required a second application, and once rinsed off, it left a slight discoloration on the fabric. The paint faded significantly on those areas treated by this product. **Rating: 4.0**

Chlorine bleach, mixed 1:5 with water and applied by spray bottle: I figured that since I had some chlorine bleach in the laundry room, I'd try my hand at mixing up a home-brew version of the previous product. It worked about as well as the store-bought kind, although not as quickly. A stronger concentrate might have worked identically, so I'll give it the same rating: **Rating: 4.0**

Chlorine bleach, mixed 1:8 with water and applied with a scrub brush: The winner, although it did require some elbow grease. The scrubbing helped work the solution into the weave, which helped it make contact with the deeper parts of the stain.

The trick here is patience ... it sometimes takes ten or fifteen minutes for the bleach to work. The worst areas had to be done two or three times. There was a little residual discoloration, and significant fading where the painted areas were treated. I recommend soaking all the fabric, not just the parts that got mildewed, because otherwise it's very easy to see the parts that got spot-treated because they're much whiter than the adjacent sections (except for the specific areas that were worst affected by the mildew stain). I also recommend using rubber gloves on your hands to avoid skin irritation. I didn't, and wished I had later when the chlorine left reddened areas on my fingers that looked a little like first-degree burns. **Rating: 4.5**

Figure 26.
After the mildew treatments ... (almost) just like new

7. Tuning your Tent

This chapter deals with getting the most out of your tent's structure. Over the years, I've noticed several tents that didn't look as good as they should have. Their fabric sagged, their poles swayed unsteadily in a wind, and, in general, they looked unhappy. And no wonder ... a tent that's unusually slack is not as secure against winds as one that's been well pitched. It also is more prone to leaking, especially if the fabric is so slack that water can collect in it. And finally, fabric that flaps and "luffs" in wind takes a lot more abuse than it's designed for. In fact, aside from UV deterioration, luffing is about the only seriously destructive force that a fabric is likely to encounter, because it repeatedly shock-loads the fibers. If the tent is dirty, all those little dirt particles can get into the fabric's weave and start grinding away at the fibers as the cloth luffs. So if you want your tent to last its longest and perform at its best, you need to eliminate that slackness.

There are basically three types of frames for large wall tents, and they each have their idiosyncrasies. Let's start with the simplest ... a center pole (or, in the case of a wedge or "bell" type, two center poles) and perhaps a ring, but no side poles. Slackness in these tents is almost always due to a center-pole that's too short.

"How can it be too short?" I hear you ask. "It was fine the last time I set up!" Well, that was then, and this is now. Over the years, the fabric might have stretched to the point where you now have a tent that's slightly bigger than the one you purchased. Or the center pole may be too short because it's sitting in a slight depression in the ground ... or the entire tent site might be slightly concave. No matter how hard you pull on the perimeter of the tent at the bottom, you're not going to make that slackness go away. The cure is to carry a few little squares of wood to use as shims. Make them out of 1" pine (which is actually ¾" thick) or ¾" plywood (which really is ¾" thick). Mine are about 4" square, but just about any dimension works as long as it's bigger than the base of the pole. The advantage of bigger pieces is that you can place them where you want your pole to be and then stand on the edges of the wood with your two feet, thereby holding the shim in place as you lift on the center pole and reposition it over the shim. On longer camping events, I've sometimes found it necessary to start with one shim (for reasons I'll explain shortly) and add another shim or two as the days go by, to adjust for the fabric gradually stretching under load.

I often start with one shim because I usually make my center poles a teeny bit short. If I'm setting up on an area which is slightly domed, instead of concave, a center-pole of exactly the right length would actually end up being a little too long. This can cause slack, too, in some designs. To understand why, try this little thought experiment. Start with a simple cone tent with one center pole. We'll mentally pull all the stakes out at the bottom. Now we'll put them all back in again, this time in a circle that's only half the circumference of the last one. Now when we raise the center pole as high as it will go, we'll have tension in those parts of the cloth that go from the stakes to the peak of the tent, but everything between the stakes will be sloppy-loose. That's the same sort of uneven tension pattern you get with a center-pole that's too long. So to make everything nice and tight, you'll have to re-set all those perimeter stakes to the greatest possible circumference, so that the skirt will be tensioned all the way around, and then raise the center pole last.

When all of this is being done, the guy ropes (if there are any) should be slack. You want to be tensioning the fabric, not the ropes. Only when everything looks snug all the way around should you tighten the guy ropes, and then only enough to "lock in" the tension you've already achieved. If the tent is well engineered and its fabric is snug, it really doesn't need a lot of tension on the ropes to shrug off the wind.

A subset of this first category is the round pavilion that uses a ring for making the eave rigid (I'm using the word "eave" to denote the part of the tent where the conical roof stops and the more-or-less vertical wall begins). It's especially important here to start with the guy ropes slack. If these ropes are tight to begin with, it's quite possible to lift up on the center pole until the canopy is tight as a drum and still not be able to tension the sides. The solution is to loosen the ropes and lift on the center pole until all the tent is tensioned ... canopy, sides, and all ... and then put enough shims under the center pole to maintain that tension. Then go outside and tighten the ropes -- again, just enough to lock in the adjustment without putting any additional tension on the canopy.

The next category of tents includes those with side poles. For tension problems above the eave-line, everything in the previous paragraphs also applies to this style. If your canopy looks good and your sidewalls are too slack, please understand that it's the side poles that govern the tension of the sidewalls, and there's not too much you can do about it. If the tent has sloping sidewalls, check to make sure that the base is staked out properly. Most of the problems here consist of the tent's bottom being not being pulled out far enough, although uneven ground can play havoc here, too. If you're camping in cow pastures, where those critters leave little craters everywhere, you might have to bring along a few more shims to make everything even.

Also, if your sidewalls hang off a rope threaded through loops in the canopy, check to see if there isn't too much slack in that rope. You don't want so much tension in that rope that it "gathers" the base of the canopy, but you don't want it too loose, either. How can you tell when too much is too much? Adjust the rope before the sidewalls are hung. Start with it completely slack (as in "untied"). When the skirt of the canopy is snug and tensioned, start adjusting the rope so as to remove all the slop from it without affecting the canopy skirt's tension. Tie it off there, reflecting that life is change, nothing is permanent, and you'll probably have to re-adjust it by and by. This rope, by the way serves two purposes: it provides something to hang the sides from, and it helps limit the amount of tension on the skirt of the roof itself. It's usually when it ages at a different rate than the roof (usually because it's made of a different material) that it starts to cause trouble.

The third type of tent uses a completely rigid frame, with the fabric taking almost no tension. Tension problems on this sort of tent are often the hardest to sort out, because they usually indicate a mismatch between the dimensions of the fabric and those of the frame. Curing them involves re-working the frame or the fabric (usually the frame). While it's true that the fabric isn't working as hard as it would in a true tension structure, it's still important that the fabric be snug ... not only for look's sake, but to increase the longevity of the tent, and to prevent the problem from getting worse. If the cover is loose, the wind luffs the fabric, the fabric weakens and stretches, becoming looser, so the wind can luff the fabric even more, which makes the fabric stretch even more ... and this stretch is more serious than the usual stretching you get with natural fabrics, because it's a sign not of the fibers accommodating themselves to climactic conditions but of the fibers giving up the fight entirely.

Since I mentioned stretching, I might as well mention that tents made entirely of synthetic fibers (of which Nylon is by far the greatest offender) can be very temperature unstable. They can shrink when warm and expand when cold. If the tent frame is made of steel, the steel will shrink when cold and expand when warm. Do we see a problem here? So a certain amount of slack may be unavoidable. But in windy conditions, the fabric will certainly be taking a beating; it will leak before its time and will eventually expire prematurely. If you have such a beast, it may help to attach the fabric parts to the frame with elastic fasteners like bungees or shock cord, to allow the fabric to change dimension without becoming too slack.

There's an additional category of tension structures that can have problems. It includes sunshades, either the dining-fly type or the "BC" style of sunshades prevalent in the western United States. Since the frames for these consist almost entirely of vertical poles, there are really only three problems that they can have:

1. The guy ropes are too slack, or aren't exerting enough force on the sunshade. More often than not, they aren't staked out sufficiently far from the base of the tent. When I see a "BC" with a really saggy ridge section, the cause is invariably guy-rope stakes that are too close to the tent. I know that when those ropes go 'way out there, they get in the way of traffic, but it's better to pitch the whole sunshade back a little farther, and hang flags on the ropes.

2. If the poles on the "BC" sunshades are out of line with each other, or if the bottoms are staked out asymmetrically, you'll get a lot of funny diagonal wrinkles. The solution is to pull up one side of the sunshade's bottom, diddle with the adjustments on the ropes until the poles are all vertical and in line not only with each other but also with the staked-down bottom side. The wrinkles are always in the direction of the greatest tension, so you loosen the guy ropes attached to the poles on either end of the wrinkle, and tighten the other ropes attached to that section. Then stake down the last side. You can avoid a lot of this by raising all the poles first, adjusting the ropes so the "roof" part is all pretty and tight, and staking down the bottom last – first one side, then the other. For maximum tension, remember to stake down each side first at the corners – not at the flap (if there is one) but at the stake loop on the seam that runs from the top of the side pole to the ground. Then stake down the center, pulling outward as much as possible before you drive the stake in. Finally, stake down the remaining stake loops and the flaps.

3. If you have good tension between the center poles, and also between the side poles on each side, but you still have a lot of slack in the area between the side pole "shoulder" and the ridge, the sides need to be re-staked. But here's the trick: stake down the two corners, grab the stake loop at the center of each side, and pull it outward as far as you can – at least six inches to a foot, depending on the side of the sunshade. You'll notice that the sag disappears like magic. It's especially important to do this if you have three center poles, since this extra tension is what keeps the fabric attached to the central center pole (you know what I mean) when the

wind picks up. There's a fuller explanation of this often-neglected procedure in Appendix B, later in this book.

PART TWO: Living in Your Tent

in which is explained the arts
of setting up camp, furnishing
your tent, and storing your stuff
for the next year

8. Situating the Campsite

You can have the best tent in the world and still have a terrible time camping. The tent is only a small part of the total environment of the campsite, the other elements of which you may not have much control over. The secret to success in camping, as in life itself, is to attend to the things that you can control and do what you can to minimize the effect of the things you can't control.

The Campsite

This may be one of those areas where you don't have much control. If you've been assigned an area, you'll have to camp there. But at least you can situate yourself in the best possible part of your assigned spot.

If rain is expected (or even if it's not), try to locate yourself on terrain that won't be flooded. In other words, don't be the lowest thing around. Make sure that there is adequate drainage, too. Somehow, all those jokes about "running water in your camp" get to be real old, real quick. A pocket-sized level, perched atop a tent pole laid on the ground, can give you accurate data about which way the ground slopes, a condition that often deceives the eye. For laying out building sites, contractors use a special kind of level called a "line level" which hangs from a string stretched out over the area you are testing. For critical work, this type is probably more accurate than the level-on-a-tent-pole setup, but it's less convenient to set up and use.

In areas of wind, try to situate yourself so that your back is to the prevailing wind. How can you tell which way the wind usually blows? Look for the way some of the trees are leaning. Or ask the locals. In most parts of the country, the strongest winds are usually from the west, but there are too many variables --- local storm patterns, local topography, and so on -- to take any particular direction for granted. For example, if you're camping in a canyon, the wind is probably going to follow the canyon's length, rather than blow across it. If you're at the base of a mountain, expect fairly strong breezes in the evening coming from air coming down the mountain. If you have any doubts about your tent's ability to weather the winds, attach some wind lines to its peak when you set up. You can leave them hanging loose until the wind picks up, at which point they can be staked down.

You'll also want to know which way the wind likes to blow when you orient yourself with respect to the toilets. I'm sure that while authenticity freaks will want to put their camps directly downwind of the toilets to heighten the medieval redolence of their campsites, everybody else will want to do the opposite.

Another factor to consider is sun. If you have a partial-wall sunshade, it's worth considering how you want to orient to maximize the shade at those times of the day that you most need it.

Savvy campers already know that setting up in the trees will keep you cooler than tents set up elsewhere. But examine the ground carefully to be sure those trees won't be dripping sap or dropping branches on you. In fact, try not to camp directly under trees if you can, because you'll get dripping from the branches long after the rain has past...not to mention the occasional falling of the branches themselves, either of which can ruin your day. And the shade from the tree is not likely to be directly under the tree, unless you're camping near the equator.

It should also go without saying that you want the campsite to be level. If that's impossible, at least arrange the beds inside so that your head is at the high point. I usually bring pieces of wood in various sizes so I can shim up tables (especially the kitchen tables) to be level.

If the stay is to be a long one, you will find that small stones under the rugs and ground cloth will appear to grow over time, until they seem to be large rocks. So take a rake and a broom with you and groom the area as much as you can before you lay down the ground cloth.

Noise control

If noise doesn't bother you, consider yourself blessed, and read no further. But if you're like me, you'll select your campsite so as to maximize your isolation from:

1. **Roads.** Particularly on the day of set up, you can count on cars using the roads well into the wee hours of the morning. Roads mean cars. Cars mean car doors. Doors mean slamming. If the area is very dry, it also doesn't take much traffic to create a lot of dust, so those with sensitivities to dust (or those who like to keep their tents clean) usually like to keep themselves some distance from the road.

2. **Privies.** Port-a-potty doors have amazing acoustical carry when slammed. And you can be sure that port-a-potties will be used all night long. Remember that if you camp twice as far from the port-a-potties, you will get only a quarter of the noise.

Speaking of privies, you'll find that another drawback of being close to privies (in addition to their aroma) is that there will be a lot of traffic going to and from them. It may be nice to live by the side of the road and be a friend to man, but you'll be a lot friendlier if you take that traffic into account and leave the pathways clear for them. It's easy to say "I was here first!" but when you argue against a full bladder or queasy stomach, you almost always lose.

It also helps sometimes to identify where the noisy parts of camp are. If quiet is important to you, try to contact the group or individual that will be running the show ahead of time and make a point of asking about it. It's always too late to try to establish the policy on the night you arrive. Groups and sites vary greatly in their ability to accommodate noise. If, despite your best efforts, the noise level is still too high, there are always earplugs. The best ones I've found are little foam cylinders that you compress and slip into the ear canal, whereupon they expand and seal out the noise. My biggest objection to them is that I can't hear the heralds in the morning, or the very soft beep my alarm makes.

Other Considerations

If you're camping with children, you need to be aware of any special hazards nearby – ponds, rivers, steep areas, poisonous vegetation, and critters like wasps. In fact, any of these could ruin anybody's event, but the consequences for children are usually much more severe.

There may be times when you're representing a household or group, and you're the first one there. You'll be expected to reserve enough space around you for the group. It's common courtesy to all your fellow campers not to reserve more than you need. In some areas, it's considered good form not to reserve space overnight for somebody else unless you have some physical part of that person's tent with you, such as the fabric or the poles. If it looks like you're not going to need all the space you reserved, by all means redraw your camp boundaries as soon as you can and let folks know that the space has become available. I'm obliged to note that this sort of courtesy has been getting rarer in the SCA of late, and would like to believe that it's not so much a sign of increasing rudeness as our failure to acculturate newcomers to what is expected of them.

If really inclement weather happens, it's not unusual for site owners to severely restrict the vehicle traffic on the site. That means that you may not be allowed to drive on to the site to load your stuff. In that case, the road you were trying not to camp near suddenly becomes your salvation, if it's the closest they'll let the cars get to the camping area. In situations where cars are banned, a pushcart or wagon really comes in handy. For the SCA's Thirty Year Celebration, I made one out of a shipping crate, two pieces of scrap pipe (for the handles), and two old bicycle wheels. It didn't look very period, but folded up flat and lived behind the tent, covered up when not in use ... and when it

63

was needed, no one could be found to complain about its looks. I eventually replaced it with a more authentic pushcart.

If you're camping in areas that are overgrown and you'd like to have a fire, there are a few more tools you need to carry with you. The first is a scythe or "weed whip" to cut back tall grass. (I'm not talking about those powered tools, but the tool with a flat, bent blade that you swing kind of like a golf club). You'll also appreciate a lawn rake to clear away the grass you've just chopped down. Sometimes you can find folding ones that take up very little space when collapsed.

Finally, a shovel comes in handy. In a pinch, I've used one of those folding shovels called an "entrenching tool" by the folks in the military) as both a shovel and a weed whip. It got the job done, but it made me wish I'd brought the proper tools for the task. The entrenching tool doesn't take up much room, and it gets used at least two or three times a year.

9. Furnishing your Tent

Even though most tents work fine right out of the box, they can all use a few details to give them the touches of "home" and make them pleasures to live in. Let's take a look at the many small things you can do to make a tent or an encampment more comfortable.

This isn't a chapter on how to make furniture, or where to buy drapery, or how to make your kitchens more efficient. There are plenty of other places to find that sort of information, and its usefulness is highly dependent on the kind of camping you do, the authenticity you require, and the money you have to spend. Instead, I'll just cover the basics, share some observations with you about what has worked for me, and attempt to steer you from the more common mistakes.

Light

The first addition I make to my tent is a light of some sort hanging from either a bracket affixed to the center pole (on a round tent) or a chain hanging from the ridge pole (if it's an oval tent). It should be high enough to avoid collisions, and far enough away from the wooden stuff to eliminate the fire hazard. There are several styles of hangars, from the ones that just sort of loop around the center pole and rely on the weight of the lamp to keep them in one place to the ones that are physically tied or bolted to the pole. I don't like the first category very much, because when the wind comes up and the tent starts shaking, a lot of that vibration travels right down the center pole and dislodges the hanger. But if the hangers are actually tied to the pole, that's far less likely to happen.

The higher the lamp is, the better a light-colored roof will help disperse the light, because you're effectively enlisting the roof cloth as a reflector. And as Peter Barclay points out, the higher the lamp, the less likely that you're going to cast shadows on the walls of the tent that reveal more of your personal activities than you would care to.

What kind of lamp? That's really up to you and the people you're camping with. In the western United States, where fire danger is uncommonly high in the summer, many areas require that all flames be enclosed in metal or glass. Other less combustible areas probably won't have this requirement, but it's a good idea nonetheless.

In our camp, we often use kerosene lamps (called paraffin lamps in the UK) because the fuel is cheaper than candles. One of the problems with them, though, is that they can be messy to fill, even with a funnel. Trying to guess how much oil a lamp can take without spilling over can be challenging, particularly when it's getting dark.

The Coleman company makes a nifty little device for filling their white-gas camp stoves. It consists of a red nozzle which screws onto a can of Coleman fuel. The nozzle is designed so that when the level of the fuel reaches the bottom of the nozzle, the fuel stream shuts off. Ergo, no overfilling and spillage.

So what does this have to do with oil lamps? Well, this nozzle also fits onto the top of some of the brands of lamp oil available at your local grocery/hardware/drugstore. I guess that a lot of these brands use the same bottle supplier, because the nozzle fits a lot of these bottles.

If you use a lot of kerosene lamps, it might be worth buying "deodorized" kerosene instead. It's essentially the same stuff, only unscented and a lot cheaper. It can probably be found in your local hardware store. The Coleman nozzle won't fit onto the can, but we buy it by the gallon and transfer it into an old Coleman fuel container or into empty lamp oil bottle (depending on how long the tourney is). Some people also like to use charcoal lighter fluid as lamp fuel, claiming that it burns cleaner. I tried it, but didn't notice any difference. It's also more expensive.

Figure 27. A hurricane lamp wind baffle

There are also little wind baffles that you can buy that perch on the top of hurricane lamp chimneys. They do a wonderful job of keeping the lamps from blowing out. Sadly, these little jewels are becoming harder to find in most hardware stores, but the ones way out in the country may still have them (or at least know what you're asking about). If your search comes up dry, you can make your own by punching or drilling a lot of ¼" holes in the bottom of a tuna fish can (or any other kind of can that fits comfortably over the chimney). Then turn the can upside down, and you have a perfectly serviceable wind baffle. The home-made ones don't work as well as the store-bought kind, but function adequately in most conditions.

In areas where we aren't allowed to use flame illumination at all, we hang battery-operated electric lights suitably disguised. For those few times when nothing less than tons of candle-power will do, we carry a propane-fueled lantern, but we hardly ever use it.

Figure 28. A home-made wind baffle

It goes without saying that the best time to find your candles and set up your lantern is before it gets dark. It's equally obvious that there are going to be plenty of times when you get to the site in the wee hours, and have enough trouble locating the flashlight you need to find the candles. It's times like that when we break out the propane lantern, because the lantern itself, with its propane bottle, is large enough to locate easily, and doesn't require any matches to fire up. But we try to keep the illumination level as low as possible, in deference to those neighbors who are disturbed by bright lights.

If you are one of those people who dislike bright lighting around you, here's a countermeasure that you can take: Get some cheap draperies (or, if you're well-heeled, expensive draperies) and hang them on the inside of your tent's side walls. Try to leave a gap of an inch or so between the two fabrics. For this modest increase in the stuff you lug around, you get three benefits:

- Those headlights that someone is shining on your tent shine through the outer layer but are stopped by the inner layer, resulting in a darker interior without great fluctuations in brightness.
- If your tent is illuminated from within, the drapes keep your silhouette from being detailed clearly, providing entertainment for all the world to see. If privacy is important to you, this feature alone makes the extra drapery worth the trouble.
- The added layer imparts a certain amount of acoustic and thermal insulation to the tent. It's not much, but it's arguably better than nothing.

An inner layer was often seen on illustrations of period tents, probably for precisely these reasons, plus the timeless one that dictates the usage of fabrics that are better then those of your neighbor: "If you've got it (expensive material, that is), flaunt it."

Ground Cloths and Carpeting

Whenever you're camping, I heartily recommend you use some sort of a ground cloth to act as a vapor barrier between you and the ground. It can be as cheap as the vinyl you get by the roll at construction supply houses or as elaborate as a custom-fitted cloth tailor-made for your pavilion. Sod flaps by themselves are not enough to keep out the wet, because most of the moisture is coming up from the ground beneath the tent, not from outside. It doesn't take much to get the bedding wet, and once that happens, you are practically guaranteed to have an unhappy campout.

Another thing that adds class to your tent is carpeting. Carpets disguise tacky ground cloths, provide a comfortable surface for your bare feet in the morning, and contribute their own mite to the insulation of the tent.

But carpets can be hazards, too, particularly if you're using slick plastic ground cloths underneath them. To minimize this, choose a ground cloth material that resists this sort of slippage, or use the sort of anti-skid mat that are commonly used between carpets and bare floors. Or, if you're using cheap carpet and cheap ground cloths, drive some nails through them and into the ground, particularly around the perimeter, to keep the carpet steady.

For carpeting, look in thrift stores or salvage companies. A carpet with a huge stain on one side is fine for camping, particularly if you're putting a bed there to hide the stain. Or look for cheap lengths of felt (natural or artificial, although I feel a lot more comfortable with the natural stuff due to its natural fire resistance).

Other Stuff

Another thing we keep in our tourney chest, even if we don't use it, is mosquito netting. It doesn't take up much room, but if the skeeters are out there it can make all the difference in comfort.

We also carry a lot of S-hooks. You hang them from the ring, spokes, or ring-tethering ropes (on a round tent), or from the rope that you hang the sidewalls from (if your tent has such a rope). Then you hang the object of your desire on the remaining hook of the S-hook. If the load is heavy, get the hook as close as possible to a side pole to avoid distorting the roof at that point.

If you have a very large tent, you'll probably want to bring extra sheets and ropes to partition off parts of it as separate rooms.

To complete our tent, and make it more than just a tent, we also have weather-hardy versions of our personal banners, a doorbell that people can shake to announce themselves, pennants or banners for the peak poles, and line flags to help avoid those accidents that can jeopardize both tent and pedestrian.

Furniture and Storage

Maybe it's a measure of my advancing years, but I am a firm believer in having a bed that's off the floor. If you want to go this route, you have a variety of choices, from a simple folding camp cot to an elaborately carved rope-suspension double bed. When I'm camping with my wife, the solution that works the best for me is a pedestal made of four slotted boards assembled in the form of two Xs, topped by a piece of 4' x 6' plywood hinged to fold into thirds. Together, they form a pedestal that's familiar to most people who have set up a waterbed. Stuff can easily get stored under the bed, except in the center where the two Xs touch. That's where we put the tent storage bags, pole ties, and the other stuff we won't be needing for the duration of the event. The hinged top folds down to fit into a 2' x 4' bag, about 2 ½" thick, and the boards go into another bag that is 4' long, about 1' wide,

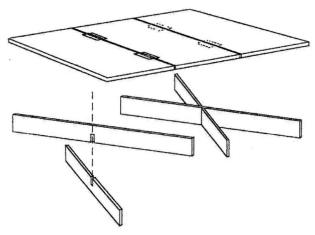

Figure 29. A fold-up camp bed

and three inches thick. It's hard to beat this bed for portability.

When I'm by myself, I take either an army cot or my twin-size rope bed.

All these beds are supplemented by foam mattresses at least three inches thick. Others swear by air mattresses. They serve the same benefits of insulation and cushioning that the foam

69

mattresses do, and pack down smaller. If you go that route, make sure you have a small pump to inflate it, and a kit to mend any punctures that may occur.

Speaking of insulation, it's worth reminding folks what the insulation values of sleeping bags really mean. When you buy a sleeping bag rated at "Zero Degrees Fahrenheit" (-7 degrees Celsius), that doesn't mean that you'll be kept comfortable at that temperature. It only means that you'll be kept alive. So make sure that your bag's rating is far below the minimum temperature you expect to encounter.

A table and chair is also a part of my tent whenever possible. If I have to write something, it somehow seems far more civilized to be able to sit down while doing it. A table is also a good place to put a lamp, but only if it, and the table, is stable and not susceptible to tipping over if the table is bumped accidentally. And, of course, the tent will be personalized over time with the stuff that reflects your interests. Folks with babies bring baby stuff, musicians bring musical instruments, and fighters bring armor and weapons. One advantage of smaller tents, in fact, is that you can truthfully say "But, honey, we don't have *room* for that!"

Speaking of room, I've made many boxes for storing and transporting the stuff we use. In nearly every case, I've designed the boxes be strong enough to be used as seats in camp. Some even have built-in cushions or padding at the top. The more boxes we have like this, the fewer chairs we have to carry.

Kitchen tents

If you're part of a large household, or camping for an extended period, it might pay to establish a separate tent just for preparing food. Since preparing means cooking, and cooking means fires and flame sources, it's worth making sure that this tent, at least, is made of flame retardant materials. You'll need tables and shelves, of course. I recommend that if you have breakables, don't store them on hanging shelves ... use hanging baskets instead. Likewise, don't put a set of shelves directly against a wall, because tent walls are likely to move, and a good gust of wind could push against the wall and knock the shelf over. Instead, make sure that there's a pole or at least a goodly amount of space between the shelf and the cloth wall.

It's wise to use a gray-water bucket to collect your dirty dish-water, stale beer, and so on. Make sure that it's well marked, and that it has a cover. I use the seven-gallon buckets that wall-patching plaster comes in, since they doesn't have to be food-grade, and they actually are colored gray, so there's no mistaking them for the white ones we store fresh wash water in.

Safety Stuff

No camp is complete without the following safety equipment, even if it's just you in your pup tent:

- First aid kit, including not only the usual stuff but any medication that you might have a special need for, like anti-venom stuff for bee stings.
- Fire extinguisher, if you have a fire, or candles, or anything that burns. The most basic fire extinguisher is a five-gallon bucket of water or sand, or a fire blanket. If you use wax-base fire logs, white gasoline stoves, or the like, remember that water doesn't work well on these fires; you should be carrying a small "A-B" fire extinguisher readily available at hardware stores, auto parts stores, or your local mega-mart.
- Line flags for all your guy ropes. I know I mentioned this before, but this is important. Tripping on guy ropes in the dark is both painful and preventable.
- Information. Make sure you know where the security and first-aid people can be found. Make sure your kids and the rest of your household know, too, so they can go there (or take you there if you're unconscious).

One last tip

This tip alone may pay for the cost of this book over the next two years. Are you ready? It goes like this:

Always carry a woolen blanket with your tourney gear.

That's it.

You don't have to be told that it's a good idea when it's cold and every bit of bedding is useful. But it also comes in handy when the weather is hot, because that's when you use it to wrap your ice chest. It's just as useful in keeping heat out as it is in keeping heat in. Result: the ice lasts longer ... often much longer. I've had a block of ice last three days, even when the temperatures topped out well over 100° Fahrenheit (37° Celsius), in the same ice chest that used to poop out after two days in the same climate.

The wool blanket is always in my car, anyway, along with a first aid kit and a fire extinguisher for use in roadside emergencies. So it's no trouble to take these articles out of the trunk along with the other gear when I'm setting up and leave them in camp, where they might be needed.

10. Painting Your Tent

Many people like to paint their tents, because it's often the easiest way to put their device (or some other elaborate graphic) on their tents. Others want to recreate the type of "architectural" painting one sees on depictions of period tents. It's probably the most effective way to give an encampment that extra note of authenticity without acquiring more stuff to set up and take down. And let's face it ... is there any better way to wake up in the morning than opening your eyes to Gothic tracery backlit by the rising sun?

Most of the earliest depictions of period tents showed the paint following the roof's seam lines, suggesting that one purpose of the paint was to help seal the seams against leakage. But it wasn't long before paint was used solely as a decorative device, disregarding the seams in favor of evoking the arches, columns, and decorative carving of buildings. The effect was to stress the "verticality" of the tent, drawing the eye skyward as the lines of Gothic architecture do. The addition of "architectural" details -- arches, columns, and the like -- may have been seen as a natural outgrowth of this earlier, necessary use of paint. However it happened, architectural details form the bulk of the painting details we see on depictions of period tents, and re-creators find them a distinctive way to make their tents unique and period-looking.

If you want to paint your tent, the very first thing you must do is obtain some more of the same type of material that your tent is made of. Each type of fabric is unique in its ability to hold paint, and it behooves you to experiment on scrap pieces before you apply paint to your tent. Tent manufacturers are usually happy to provide you with scrap, which they generally have in abundance. So don't hesitate to take advantage of this opportunity.

Tents made of Sunforger or other all-cotton canvases can take just about any kind of paint. The only danger here is that they tend to absorb a lot of paint. That's a good thing, because it allows the paint to soak directly into the fibers of the cloth and results in a long-lasting application. But its downside is that if you're not careful, it can absorb more of the paint than you want, and all the colors come out a bit darker or more intense than you'd like.

Another problem with fabric paint is that under some circumstances, it can bleed and run. The usual cure for this is heat-setting, where your painted canvas is subjected to drying in an industrial dryer for a certain length of time. This method has worked for me, but not for others. Some people have had good luck with setting the paint using an electric iron, but others haven't ... another good reason to experiment on scrap fabric and verify that your paint responds well to this treatment. A third option is to buy an additive from your supplier that sets the paint without the use of heat. I have had no trouble with using the additive (other than the fuss of adding miniscule amounts of this to the paint and hoping I added just enough, but not too much). For the record, all of my experience has been with Versatex fabric printing paint, and the fixative that is recommended for it.

Most tents which use a cotton-polyester blend with an acrylic top coat take well to artist's acrylic paints. The paints are easy to apply, flexible, and reasonably durable. They come in two varieties. The first type is a "high-viscosity" formulation that mimics the consistency of oil paints. This type works well for those who are brushing directly on the canvas, but can't be airbrushed on, because you'd have to dilute it too much to get the airbrush to accept it.

A better match for top-coated fabric is the second variety of acrylic paint, known as a "medium viscosity" paint. This uses more pigment and less thickeners, which is what you want when you're painting on tent canvas. Even thinned to the point where an airbrush can use it, it does a pretty good job of covering the fabric. It's important to use a thinning medium specifically designed for air-brush use. Even thinned down, this paint is still a bit thicker than the stuff that usually goes through an air-brush, so make sure your compressor and nozzle arrangement is up to the job. If you're silk-screening a fabric with an acrylic top coat, you could really go with either a "high-viscosity" or a "medium-viscosity" medium, although you might get better results with a high-viscosity formulation, since it seems to behave more like silk-screen ink. It's wise to buy a little of each type of paint, and see which one works better with your fabric, your screen, and your technique.

If you're using stencils, the higher-viscosity paint may work better because it resists "wicking" under the stencil.

Whatever your canvas, there are many ways to apply pigment. What follows is, in no particular order, are some of the techniques I've developed, along with observations that people have passed on to me on what methods and tricks worked best for them.

If you're using a stencil and air-brushing the paint on, it helps to have some way of sticking the stencil material to the canvas. Otherwise, the blast of air might force the stencil off the canvas, causing particles of paint to blow underneath the stencil. I've used two methods for doing this. The first method uses double-sided tape around the edge. This stuff can be hard to come by, and tends to be expensive, but is available. The other method involves punching lost of holes around the periphery of the stencil and covering the holes with tape. When you lay the stencil on the canvas and rub on the tape, the stencil will adhere to the cloth.

A lady who uses stencils reports that she's had good luck with the sort of printer's ink that lithographers use.

How about commercial house-paint? Some people have written to tell me that they've used it with good results. Others have written to tell me that it's all flaked off after a few years (or even months). The difference in their experiences, I think, stems from the water-repellent treatment of the cloth versus the paint's ability to form a bond despite the treatment. Latex exterior house paint seems to work well if diluted one-to-one with water; this makes it penetrate more easily into the fibers, and results in a thinner coat that is less likely to crack or flake off. My advice is to use good-quality paint, and to experiment on some fabric first to get the technique down.

I don't recommend felt-pen ink dispensers like "Magic Markers," "Sharpies," "Marks-a-Lot" or other trademarked names. These tints aren't very color-stable. They fade or change hue dramatically with exposure. They tend to bleed, too.

If you have a small but intricate design, in color, that you'd like to have on your tent but don't want to paint on, there's another alternative. If you have access to a scanner, a graphics program, and a color ink-jet printer, it's possible to make iron-on decals in whatever design you can scan in. (We at Dragonwing have been using this method to print the "Warning" labels mandated by California law.) They stick well to all-cotton fabrics like Sunforger, and aren't affected by weather and washing. The only trick with applying these is to use just enough heat. Not enough heat will make the decal fail to adhere to the cloth, and too much will cook the ink and cause the colors to change a bit. So it's still a good idea to ask the manufacturer to send you some scraps to experiment with. (Of course, if you stick with a black-and-white design, you won't have that problem, and you can use a cheaper non-color ink-jet printer.)

When choosing a design to paint, keep it simple, keep it colorful, and keep it period. Simple, because you're going to be looking at it a lot as you're painting, and even more after you're done with it. Colorful, because you want it to stand out and make the strongest effect for the least paint. And period, because the whole enterprise rises or falls on how accurately it evokes the tentage of the Middle Ages. So be prepared to study as many depictions of period tents as you can find. The Internet has many web sites devoted to this, and they are worth the trouble to explore.

One last piece of advice: If you intend to paint your tent, it's best to do it while the tent is new. After a few years, a tent can accumulate dirt and oils that may affect a paint's ability to hold. Of course, paints can also be used to disguise stains and such, as I've mentioned in the chapter on repairs. But you'll still have to clean the cloth as best you can to get out as much of the dirt as possible; otherwise, the paint may adhere unevenly and leave you with even more areas in need of disguise.

11. Storing your Tent for the Winter

And all your other stuff as well

When the summer is winding down, it's time to think about putting your tourney gear to bed for the winter. What you'll need for this operation are a few of the warm, dry days that "Indian summer" gives us (or its equivalent wherever you are), a storage area that's dry and vermin-free, a piece of paper, and a pencil. The pencil and paper are for writing down all the things that need to be repaired, replaced, or replenished over the winter, so you'll be able to hit the ground running come springtime with equipment that's in top shape.

The tent

If you've got a few warm, dry days of autumn left, now's the time to wash the tent and set up so it can dry thoroughly. When it's up, you can also check over the tent and see what needs repairing ...grommets, stake loops, seams, and ties, in particular. It's also a good time to inspect ropes and stakes, to see if you have a full complement of them, and if they can be expected to deliver another year's worth of service.

Look over your poles very carefully, especially if you intend to store them outside. This is probably as good a time as any to re-finish them, if the finish is starting to get beat or if you used a wax or oil finish that requires periodic replenishing. If possible, store the poles vertically, with the bottoms away from contact with moisture or the ground so the moisture doesn't get drawn into the end grain by capillary action. If that's not possible, store them horizontally, making sure that they are well supported so they don't bend in storage. I find it helps if you keep them tightly bundled. If it looks like they're bending anyway, you can reduce the effect by rotating them half a turn, once a month or so.

As you do your inspections, write down everything that needs attention. From this list, you can generate a shopping list of things you'll need for your renovations, and a project list. One of the benefits of doing this in the fall is that you'll probably have a lot more items on your two lists than you thought you would, and you'll be glad to have a long stretch of time when the equipment isn't going to be in use.

(Of course, one of the downsides is that, since you won't be using the equipment for a while, it's easy to put all the projects off, resulting in a quick, panicked review of the list the following spring, three days before you next use the stuff. This latter condition seems to be my particular failing ... in fact, my friends might claim that it's my usual operating procedure. This year will be different, though. Really.)

When the tent is ready to come down, first make sure that it is absolutely and completely dry ... the ropes and stakes, too. You're going to be putting it away for a long time, and the last thing you want is a mildew farm. If your tent or ropes are made of synthetic materials, you've already taken a great step in reducing mildew simply by washing the pieces, because mildew won't survive on synthetics but have no problem subsisting on the organic dirt and crud on them. Once you're sure the pieces are dry, store them in a cool dry area. If you're not sure of the water-tightness of your storage area, it doesn't hurt to stuff the pieces into plastic "lawn and leaf" bags and taping the bags shut.

If you have steel or iron stakes, give them a light coat of wax or WD-40 to keep them from rusting. (Incidentally, that's what WD-40 was invented for. The WD stands for Water Dispersant, and it was presumably the fortieth compound that was tested for that application. But you knew that.)

The Rest of the Equipment

It's not only tents that need periodic maintenance. Wooden furniture needs to be refinished from time to time, particularly if it sees a lot of exposure to the elements or if it's been finished with stuff that requires replenishing (notably waxes and oils). Now is the time to do it, before dry winter conditions suck out whatever moisture has been keeping the furniture from cracking or loosening. If the piece has hinges, oil them now while the piece is in the garage and the oilcan is handy.

As collapsible furniture ages, its pieces expand and contract in ways that may not have been intended, resulting in poor (or, in extreme cases, impossible) fit between them. Now that you have your tourney gear at home, you can bring out the utility knives and sandpaper and chisels and remove whatever you need to remove to make all the pieces fit nicely together again. Having restored the piece, refinishing it (or at least the areas where raw wood has been exposed) will stabilize it so your perfect fit can be maintained.

Go through the kitchen stuff, and see what could use a good clean before it gets put away. By performing this task now, we often find and discard that apple that slipped down into the crockery, which would otherwise have made some interesting transformations over the winter. (I once heard of somebody who neglected this vital step and found the remains of a dead mouse in her kitchen gear one spring. It had evidently gotten in during the last tourney of the season and had the entire winter to decompose and stink up the kitchen chest. You have been warned.) We also replenish stocks of salt and sugar and such, but wait until spring before re-stocking the more perishable herbs and spices. Stuff that needs to be mended can be put aside. All the linen gets washed — the bed linens, too — before it's packed away for the winter.

Make sure that the place you're storing propane bottles and tanks is adequately ventilated. A very small leak over a period of months can result in a large amount of accumulated gas and a correspondingly large chance of everything going *boom.*

Since we often use sites that don't allow firewood collecting, we bring our own with us. We usually make sure we have half a cord or so set by in the autumn, so it can season over the winter and be fairly dry and ready to burn by springtime. Unseasoned wood is generally a lot cheaper than the seasoned stuff, since you're not paying to have somebody store it for you, but you have to anticipate your needs well in advance. (This comes as no news to those of you who customarily heat with wood and have plenty of it on hand, but I've included it for the benefit of those who don't usually keep much wood around.)

Drain all your water containers, rinse them out with a weak chlorine solution to sterilize them, and make sure they're dry when you store them. Or do what we do, which is re-fill them and keep them around as "emergency water" if you live in an area where the water supply becomes undependable under emergency conditions such as floods, earthquakes, or hurricanes. You have to replace these emergency stores on a regular basis anyway, so you might as well use it as your tourney water supply, too.

We suggest you use the winter hiatus to scrape all the wax and soot out of our lanterns, replace the wicks in the oil lamps, and re-stock your supply of candles and lamp oil. This serves two purposes: the equipment will be ready for spring's tourney season, and it will also be ready for use around the house in the event that a winter storm knocks out your electrical power. (One of the advantages of living in an SCA household is that one tends to be ready for such things. When we lost power after northern California's Loma Prieta earthquake of 1989, we had a lamp for every room in the house. Neighbors would see our house lit up and knock on our door to ask, "How come you're the only people on the block who have power?")

PART THREE:
Making a Tent

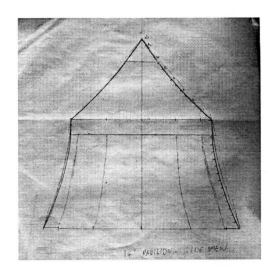

in which is explained the arts of tentmaking, tools, machines, and other useful stuff

12. Designing your Tent

If this book were written thirty years ago, this section would have been the first one, because commercial pavilion makers were few and far between and, if you wanted a tent, you usually had to make it yourself. Now there are several tentmakers making several styles and sizes, and chances are that you can buy one that will suit your needs. But there will still be those who want a tent that is unique, and those who want to save some money by making it themselves. The following chapters are for them. But they are also for those of you who've bought a commercially made tent, and want to know something about how their tents were designed and the choices the designer had to make in the design process.

Choosing a pavilion design is a lot like buying a tent, so go back to that chapter and study it well. The same principles apply. Before you settle on a pavilion design, talk with a few people who have made their own. Most will be more than willing to bend your ear about them, including what they would have done differently the second time around. If there is a design you're particularly attracted to, ask to help them set it up and take it down. See how many people, and what sort of effort it takes -- it may not suit your own particular tourneying style.

This book will not cover making any particular styles of tent, and will not have detailed plans or patterns. There are plenty of resources for those, mainly on the Internet. Instead, we'll discuss some general principles of design and construction, followed by chapters on specific aspects of tentmaking that the other sources don't have the space to cover, or thought you already knew.

If a round "arming" pavilion or Viking tent is your cup of mead, read the articles on these styles in the *Known World Handbook,* an SCA publication. There are also descriptions of pavilions in their Compleat Anachronist booklet *Pavilions of the Known World,* in back issues of the *Elf Hill Times,* and in other local publications. There used to be plans published by Medieval Miscellania of Virginia, and some of those might still be floating around somewhere. (The very best book I have seen on the subject is *Building a Medieval-Style Pavilion,* written by Christine Robertson and privately published in Australia.) There are also several sources on the Internet for pavilion plans and construction hints. I've listed the most important ones in Appendix A. There's no telling if they'll still be around a year from now, since web sites have a way of disappearing like Brigadoon, but doing a Google search on "Medieval Pavilion" should put you on the doorstep of the best sites. Be prepared to take a lot of time chasing down links; it will be time well spent.

You can also get plans from people who've made tents and have already done all the necessary calculations. They may have even made re-useable patterns and would be happy to share them with you. One additional advantage of this is that you can inspect their finished tent and see what modifications have to be made to the patterns to improve them.

If you can't find a set of plans that will result in the perfect tent for you, it's not too difficult to design one from scratch. First, plan on sloped sidewalls for stability in winds. Plan to cant the wall inward at least one foot for a seven-foot-high sidewall. More is better, although beyond a certain point, you are trading off interior space. Your canopy (roof) should have a pitch of no flatter than 1:4; that is, it should be at least one foot high for every four feet across. Again, more is better, particularly if your design calls for a minimum of framing to support the canopy, because rain will cause the roof to sag and collect puddles in a tent without enough roof slope. If you expect to get snowed on, a pitch of 1:2 is probably the least you can get away with. Also, the higher the roof pitch, the less critical your waterproofing becomes. (You'll notice that period pavilions were tall, with pitches of around 1:1. Besides allowing imperfectly sealed cloth to shed rain, this design feature made it easier to keep the interior cool.)

You want two doors in your tent, one in the front and one in the back. This way, you can have cross-ventilation and, if that strong wind that was blowing from the south turns into a strong wind blowing from the north, you can close off the windward door and use the leeward door instead.

Once you have the basic dimensions nailed down, draw an accurately scaled floor plan of the tent, showing how much space is available both at ground level and, if the walls are canted, at the height of the top of the furniture you intend to use in it. Draw the outline of your beds, tables, and whatnot, and see where they'll fit. Did you leave enough space for walking around? It's a lot easier to scale the tent up, or the furniture down, at this point than afterwards.

Basic Geometry for Tentmakers

It's not hard to calculate what the dimensions of your panels are going to be and how much cloth you're going to need if you recall the basics of your high school geometry.

Let's start with square tents. We can divide this shape into two sections: the roof (along with its valence, if any) and the sides. Our first critical dimension is the height of the tent, which

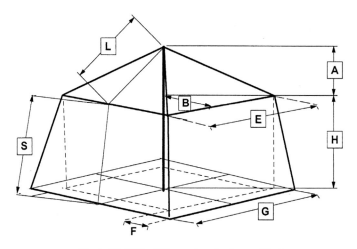

Figure 30. Critical Dimensions for Square Tents

we're going to divide into two components: the height of the sides (hereafter known as H), which is the true vertical distance from the ground to the eave line, and the remaining height from eave level up to the peak of the tent, which we'll call the roof height, or A for short.

To calculate the area of the roof, you need the roof height (A) and the length of the roof (E), along the eave. This eave length, divided by two, will be the distance from the center pole to the center of the eave. We'll call this distance B.

The length of the main roof panels (L) will be the square root of the sum of A^2 plus B^2, as Pythagoras discovered long ago. Now get out your graph paper, choose a scale that lets you keep everything on the paper, and draw a triangle with a height of L and a base of E. That's the working picture of one of your roof sides.

Now you want to see how it works with various seam layouts. There are two choices, and the one you choose will depend on the width of the fabric you want to use. You could center the main panel on the center line of the triangle you just drew, and have one or two subsidiary panels on each side to complete the side. Or you could build your side by halves, with one main seam running from eave to peak, and subsidiary panels seamed to the main pieces if you need to make more width. It really depends on what width of cloth you're using, and what will give you the most efficient use of the cloth. The latter method also presents the problem of twice as many seams converging at the peak, so you might want to avoid that if your sewing machine isn't up to the load. (Or you can use a separate cone at the peak, described below.)

You can also play around with seeing if the cut-offs you form when you trim the panels are big enough to serve as subsidiary panels.

I've found it helpful to use the first method, where the main panel is centered on the centerline of the side. However, there's a slight refinement: I make the center panels of the front and back roof sides a little wider than the ones on the sides of the roof ... maybe three or four inches. It wastes a little more cloth, but it keeps the seams of the subsidiary panels from overlapping when you seam the panel assemblies together to form the angled roof seams.

Once you've decided your panel sizes and shapes, you draw them out on your graph paper. Remember to add your seam allowances here, and adjust the width of the panels to suit. See how to nest them on the cutting table for maximum efficiency. After this, it's simply a matter of measuring out how long the panels are, and multiplying by four to arrive at the yardage needed for the entire roof.

To calculate the valance, divide the eave width E by the width of your fabric to determine how many separate pieces you need for each side. (That's the way you should cut them, rather than simply cutting one long strip from the length of the cloth. This is because some fabric stretches less along its length than its width, and you want to match the "fill" of your valance to the "fill" of the roof panels to keep the stretch identical.) Now that you know how many pieces you need, multiply by four, and multiply that figure by the depth you want your valance to hang, and the result will be the amount of cloth needed for the valance. If you're going to flare out the sides of the tent (and you should), remember to add a little extra so you can angle the ends of the valance match the angle of the sidewalls.

Now for the sides. You need three dimensions: the width of the side of the tent at the top (and that would be our old friend E), the width of the side of the tent at the ground level (which we'll call G), and the height of the tent at the eave (whose name is H).

To get the length of the sidewall panel, we need to know how much the side flares out. That's the difference between the distance from the center pole to the eave ($1/2E$) and the distance from the center pole to the base ($1/2G$). So $(1/2G) - (1/2E) = F$, right?

With our newfound value F and the help of Pythagoras, we can calculate the length of the sidewall. It will be the square root of the sum of F^2 and H^2. We'll call this value S. Again, your hem allowances have to be added to that figure, and if you're using hooks to hang the walls from an eave pole or eave rope, subtract a little to compensate for the length of those hooks.

We repeat the process with the graph paper, laying out our panels and determining how to cut them most efficiently. As we did earlier, we multiply by four. Then we add the extra amount you'll need for your door panel overlap. (I think it's this detail that most first-time tent designers forget, only to realize their error once the cloth has been obtained and the construction is well underway.)

Round pavilions are a tad more complex, but they needn't scare you. It's just a question of the tent having more than four sides. How many more? That depends on how truly round you want to be. You can go with as little as six sides, or as many as you want (although once you get beyond twelve sides, they all look pretty round to me.) The determining factor is usually the cloth width you have to work with, and how much seaming you want to do to form the individual side panels.

Since we're working with only approximations of circles, it's tricky to determine the actual circumference of the tents. So I've provided the table below, which does much of the complicated mathematics for you. To understand why the table is necessary, let's compare a square and a circle, both with a distance across of one meter. The circumference of the square will be 4 meters, while the circumference of the circle will be 3.1416 meters. Quite a difference!

Number of sides	Circumference ratio	Ratio of Side Panel Width To Tent Diameter
4	4.0000	1.0000
6	3.4641	0.5774
8	3.3137	0.4142
10	3.2492	0.3249
12	3.2154	0.2679
14	3.1954	0.2282
16	3.1826	0.1989
18	3.1739	0.1763
20	3.1677	0.1584
22	3.1631	0.1438
24	3.1597	0.1317
26	3.1570	0.1214
28	3.1548	0.1127
True Circle	3.1416	

A six-sided figure will approximate a circle a little more closely; the ratio of its diameter to its circumference will be 3.4641. Closer, but still no cigar. As the polygon morphs into a figure with more and more sides, you'll see how the ratio in the middle column moves more and more to 3.1416.

But it's the right hand column that really gives you the information you need. It's the ratio of the panel width to the diameter of the circle at the base or eave (or any point in between, for that matter.) (By "diameter" I mean the distance across the polygon, measured from flat side to flat side, because it's the dimension that's truly important when trying to figure out panel sizes.)

Here's how you use the table. Let's say you're designing a tent that's fifteen feet in diameter at the base, and is twelve-sided. You look at the table and find that the ratio of the diameter to the panel width is 0.2679. Multiply that figure by 15, and you end up with 4.02 feet, or 48.22" as the width of your panel at the base. If your cloth is 60" wide, you've got width to spare. If your cloth is only 48" wide, you're in trouble, because there's nothing left for seam allowances. So you have the option of making the tent a little smaller, or going with a different number of side panels. If we re-design the tent to be 14' wide, we end up with a panel width of 3.75' or 45", and you're back in business.

If you really insist on that 15' diameter, you could increase the number of panels. A bit of fiddling with math tells me that you could make a 20-sided tent with individual panels of 30" or so. By cutting your panels lengthwise, you'd have a 32" piece and a 16" piece; by seaming a couple of 16" pieces together, each two lengths of fabric would yield three panels. You'd end up with more efficient use of cloth, with a penalty of 50% more seaming to do. That's the trade-off.

Now that you've got the dimension of your side panel's width at the base, use the same method to determine the width at the top, multiplying the diameter of the tent at the eave by the appropriate figure in the right-hand column of the table.

Once we've settled on the dimensions of the base and the eave, all that's left is the length of the side panels. This calculation is performed just as we did for the square tents, with the slight difference being that G and E represent the diameters at the base and eave, not the dimension across the face of the tent at those points. You find the amount of flare-out by subtracting half the diameter of the eave from half the diameter of the base. $(1/2G) - 1/2E) = F$.

We can then calculate the panel length S, which is the same formula we used for the square tents: the square root of the sum of H^2 and F^2. Armed with these dimensions, we can lay out the panel on graph paper, add the hem and seam allowances, and derive an actual cutting length for your panel. You then multiply that length by however many sides your tent has, and add whatever you want your door overlap to be (generally one extra panel each for the front and back door).

Now for the roof panels. We know the eave dimension E. We also know the roof height A. The length of our panel would then be the square root of the sum of A^2 plus B^2. Actually, it's not, but draw it that way on our graph paper. Now we'll slightly alter that picture as follows:

Find a drawing compass. Put the metal-pin arm of the compass on the apex (top) point of the panel, and expand it so the pencil arm is at either end of the eave line. Connect the two ends of the eave lines with an arc, traced directly below the eave line itself. Draw another arc roughly halfway in between the first arc and the flat base of the panel. This will represent the actual eave of the tent. Why? Because on just about every round I've seen, the canopy is connected to the frame at the ends of the eave lines, either by a ring or spokes. Those points are also where you attach guy ropes. So there is maximum tension between those points and the peak of the tent. Tension means stretch. But at the center point between those end points on the eave, the tension is at its lowest, and you won't get much stretch at all. It may even shrink a bit. After a while, you'll see that the centers of the eave seams want to ride upward, giving a sort of inverse scallop to the eave of the tent. If the valance has been cut straight, its bottom will also want to pucker. The extra bit you add will give the roof enough fabric to compensate for that, leaving the valance at an even height all the way around.

At this point, you also have the option of omitting the separate valance and extending each roof panel by the width of the valance, thereby forming the valance from the extended part of the roof panels. This may make sewing a little easier, but it doesn't allow you to engineer in that compensating curve I mentioned in the last paragraph. I also feel that the seam connecting the valance to the roof adds a bit of needed strength to that area.

Add the seam allowances for your valence (if it's not integral with the roof panel) or sidewall connection (if you're sewing the side to the roof), and you've arrived at the new, improved panel length you will use when you calculate how much fabric you'll need. Since these panels are all roughly triangular, it's worth fiddling with the layout so you can "nest" the points together as you draw the panels, saving a bit of cloth. But I would advise keeping the center-line of the panels parallel with the warp or fill of the canvas, rather than on a diagonal, to keep the stretch uniform along the panel, even if it means wasting a bit more cloth.

If you didn't use the roof panel extensions to form your valance, you'll have to calculate the amount you'll need for it, remembering that you're dividing the circumference at the eave by the width of your fabric to determine how many pieces you'll need.

Way back in Chapter One, I explained how an oval or marquee tent is basically a "stretched" version of a round or square tent. To make one, you cut the thing in half vertically, move the two halves apart, and fill the intervening space with fabric. If you want to make the most efficient use of cloth, the distance you move the two sections apart will be an even multiple of the "working" width of your fabric (that is, the width of your fabric once you have subtracted the seam allowance). Calculating the added wall and valance is the same as calculating the fabric needed for two sides and valance sections of a square tent, except that the bottom measurement of the side panels will be the same as the width at the eave. As for the roof, the panels will be the same width as the eave of the tent both at their bottom (at the eave) and at their top (at the ridge).

As for the doors, you might want to make the overlaps a little smaller than a full panel, because you can use what you cut off to make a long reinforcement for the roof area that touches the ridgepole. This reinforcement serves two purposes: it helps control stretch in an area subjected to great strain, and it prevents the ridgepole from chafing on the working layer of the fabric.

Your next step will be to build a model of your design, in a convenient scale (say, 1:10 or 1:12), by cutting out a paper representation of each and every panel in your tent, and gluing or taping them together with an overlap to represent the seam allowances. Graph paper is handy for this. The purpose of this step is twofold: Your are going to verify that the panel dimensions will work with the width of the fabric you intend to use, and you will see how the design is going to fit together, thus avoiding unpleasant surprises when you begin work on the real thing. Paper is cheaper than cloth!

If you're happy with the model, you're ready to order the fabric. Before you place the order, have somebody check your math. When you order, be sure to order an extra 10% to 15% to compensate for miscalculations and miscuts. If you end up not needing this extra amount, good on you! But you can still use it for bags, repairs, paint experiments and such.

You can also design the frame at this point, although I recommend that you hold off actually building it until the fabric parts are finished. That's because it's easier to make the final adjustment on the frame than on the fabric parts.

Incidentally, I use the term "fabric parts" in the plural, although you may wish to sew everything together. I like to make at least the walls and canopy separate, because with the relatively non-porous material I use, having a gap between the two pieces facilitates air circulation and keeps the interior cooler. It also makes the tent easier to store and carry.

If the fabric is going to contribute to the structural strength of the pavilion, make sure that those parts of the fabric that actually take the load are up to the strain. This is done in three ways: using reinforcement at stress points, "roping" seams (either by running lengths of rope through the pocket formed by the seem, or by sewing webbing over or into the seam itself), and using a heavier canvas for those load-bearing panels. With really large tents, all three methods may be used. We'll explore this further in the chapter called "Patches, Seams, and Hems."

The fine arts of cloth selection and fabric construction are covered in the next chapters, so study them well. Your finished cover should fit snugly on its frame, without sagging. Loose fabric will flutter and luff in winds, degrading the cloth by breaking down the weatherproofing and imparting shock loads to the fibers.

Constructing the frame

There are a variety of preferences in frames. Some people want lightness and convenience, others go for truly period "reconstructions" in wood, and most of us fall somewhere in between. Given this diversity, I can do no more than give you a few general principles and hints:

Be conservative and over-engineer! Allow for strong winds, rain, snow, or somebody blundering into a pole. Test the finished product by grabbing a pole and shaking like hell ... the structure should be solid.

Just how sturdy do the poles have to be? There's a great temptation to save weight by using a barely adequate pole for a job, but remember that center poles are subjected to greater loads when the tent is being set up or struck than they do while the tent is up. Unless you're real good with calculating loads, your best bet is to seek out a commercial manufacturer with a tent of similar size and style and use what he or she uses. There's a more extensive discussion of this subject in Chapter Eighteen, which also covers the types of woods that are available.

You can design poles with breakdowns, but make sure that the spliced areas are at least as strong as the rest of the pole. A good rule of thumb for a sleeve length is six times the diameter of the pole you're using.

If you're using wood, it's sometimes cheaper (and for pieces longer than eight feet, usually necessary) to rip 2" x 4" stock lengthwise for 2" x 2"s. Round stock is usually more expensive, and a diameter of at least 1-5/8" is usually required for a strength equivalent to a 2" x 2."

If you make your frame using pipe and welded corner fittings, be sure that the fittings aren't so snug that even the slightest distortion of the end will cause the fitting to seize up. Many people make this mistake. They're the ones you see beating at the joints of their pavilion frame when setting up or striking camp. They know who they are.

I recommend plastic tubing (PVC or plastic conduit) only for areas that define shape, not for members that take a load. In other words, if the pavilion won't stand if the member is removed, the member should not be plastic. The same goes for electrical conduit like EMT thin-wall. The stuff was designed to bend under load, not to resist it, so it won't be up to any serious structural task.

If your tent frame is composed of several pieces of pipe and fittings, few of which are interchangeable, then numbering or color-coding parts makes field assembly quicker and more accurate. The same goes for ropes and other small pieces. A better system, if you use synthetic rope, is to keep the ropes permanently connected to some part of the pavilion. That way, you don't need to figure out which rope goes where. (You can't use this trick with all ropes, though. I learned to my regret that some oil-impregnated ropes will stain fabric if stored together.)

I roll up my guy ropes into a loose bundle, like a lasso, and tie the bundle with a loose overhand knot to keep it organized. Ideally, you will have all the miscellaneous pieces sorted by type and stored in bags, so you can locate everything by sunset, including your hammer.

Above all, practice setting up your pavilion before the tourney, in daylight and fair weather. Get good enough at it to be proficient when conditions become more adverse.

13. Tent Fabrics

The very best fabric for period-looking tents would look just like a cotton or hemp canvas. It would be light (4 oz maximum) but strong and very opaque to light. It would repel water indefinitely, like a fabric laminated on one side with vinyl or urethane, but breathe to allow transmission of water vapor, like Gore-tex. And it would cost twenty-five cents a yard.

Unfortunately, many materials fit at least one of these requirements, but none fits all of them (particularly that last one). Every fabric represents a sort of compromise between those variables. There is no best fabric for all purposes, so what you use will depend on more on the kind of camping you do, how period you want to look, and how much weight you want to attach to safety factors such as fire-retardance and UV transparency.

Of course, the flame-retardant stuff costs more, and one of the reasons you're building your own tent may be to save money. But what is your safety worth? Moreover, suppose you want to sell the tent some time down the road. If you're selling to a private individual, there's no state law that prevents you from doing so. But a merchant may be reluctant to buy your tent because he may have to comply with local ordinances mandating flame-retardant tents for vendors.

There are a few important differences between tent fabric and garment fabric. First, remember that tents are (usually) tension structures. Therefore, shrinkage is usually not as important as stretch.

Second, tent fabrics need a certain degree of impermeability to water. This quality is achieved in various ways. To some extent, the cotton content of the fabric helps, because cotton expands as it absorbs moisture, helping to tighten the weave. Waterfastness can also be increased by treating the fabric with either a wax-based waterproofing compound (which also makes it more flammable, unfortunately) or a silicon-based water-repelling compound. (An example of the latter is Scotch-gard, although there are other products developed specifically for camping tents.) I'll talk about these treatments in a later chapter.

Third, most garment fabric has been treated with "sizing," which is basically starch or some other stiffening agent. This makes the cloth easier to sew, but is water-soluble. It's meant to get washed away after a few launderings, but that means it will also wash out after a few rains, and the stretch and handling properties of the cloth will be greatly affected, and not for the better. So you have to get the sizing out before you use the cloth for tentage.

Tentage fabrics

For your first tent (and for subsequent ones, too) I heartily recommend that you use a fabric specifically designed for tents. It should be pre-shrunk and treated for water repellence and mildew resistance. It will be far more expensive than other canvas cloths, but will pay for itself in the long run by lasting longer and being easier to handle. In most cases, you can also use cloth that's made specifically for awnings, since they're engineered to the same specifications (including, in many cases, flame-retardance).

Some people have told me that they didn't want to use expensive cloth for their first tents because they knew that the tent would be only temporary. They figured that it would be junk after a season or two, but the experience gained from making it would allow them to make a much better tent, more worthy to be made from good material. They have a point there. But those "prototype" tents never seem to get retired that quickly, and continue to be used even after the better tent is finished. Also, if you've taken the steps described in the previous chapter to heart, you'll have made a cheaper paper model of your tent that serves most of the same purposes as that prototype tent. So design that first tent well, design it to last, and make it out of a fabric that lasts.

For your first tent, and for subsequent ones as well, I recommend Sunforger, which is available in both fire-retardant and non-fire retardant finishes. (The fire-retardant finish is a bit heavier.) This fabric is commonly available, cuts easily, and sews without much trouble. It is fairly stretchy under tension, so it fares better with tents that use center poles and side poles. It repels small amounts of moisture very well, and only driving rains will force water through the material. However, if the fabric is touched on the "dry side," the water may seep through the material and drip inside; this becomes more common as the fabric ages. Its mildew resistance is pretty good, although it tends to absorb a lot of water and must be dried thoroughly before storage. When dry, it breathes very well.

If you've had some previous canvas-sewing experience, you might also consider cotton/polyester canvas. It also comes in fire-retardant and non-fire-retardant flavors. Tentmakers use the former exclusively. This fabric has an acrylic "top coat" which looks like a light coat of paint applied to the canvas. This helps seal the fabric even more against moisture, while still letting it breathe a little bit. The coating drastically reduces seep-through from driving rain, and you usually don't have to worry about anything touching the inside of the tent. The cloth's polyester content reduces any tendency to shrink or stretch, making it a better cloth for tents with rigid frames (or any other arrangement where a close fit is critical). Because it does not readily absorb water, it usually dries in a matter of hours rather than days. Its mildew resistance is very good, although it should not be packed up wet.

(Even synthetics can mildew, by the way. As I've noted elsewhere, the mildew organisms can survive and thrive by eating the organic dirt on the tent, even if the tent material itself is unpalatable to them.)

These cotton-polyester canvases were originally designed as awning material, and are expected to withstand five years of constant exposure to the elements. I have personally verified this by making a trailer cover out of it and leaving it exposed to the California's central valley's harsh summer sun and winter rains. It lasted for six years before I had to treat it with something to restore its finish.

I use a six-ounce cotton-polyester twill for my sunshades. While not treated for water repellence, it has enough cotton content to allow some swelling of the threads to reduce seepage. But it's not something I'd want to rely on in a driving rain. In tents, it's only suitable for non-load-bearing sides.

100% polyester cloths are the least susceptible to stretch, and age very well. They usually have to be treated for water repellence before they can be used for canopies (roofs) of tents, but they may fill the bill for tent sides.

Nylon cloths are undesirable for tent material, unless they have been specifically designed for tentage. There are several reasons for this. First, nylon is fairly UV-transparent; you can get a pretty good sunburn sitting in a nylon tent. Second, nylon has a negative coefficient of expansion. That is, it shrinks when warm and expends when cold. So if your tent relies on a constant tension on ropes and fabric to keep it stable and pretty-looking, nylon will not do the job for you. Finally, most nylon pack cloth is coated with a urethane coat on one side to make it moisture-proof. This coating ruins whatever "breatheability" the cloth may once have had. Nylon's sole virtue is its strength, which makes it easier for you to make a tent that's light and packs into a small space, and easier to manhandle through a sewing machine.

Most of the better nylon camping tents I've seen have a roof section made of polyester, to reduce the UV transparency of the tent. The nylon and polyester used in tents are also treated with other UV blockers to extend the life of the fabric, but the stuff from your local fabric store is unlikely to have these treatments.

In my career as a tentmaker, I've used all of the above materials, plus many others. (One of my favorites was a four-ounce polyester material called "Camplite" which I used extensively for sidewalls and even a few canopies with good results. Unfortunately, it's no longer made.) All these tents had their good and bad points, but generally, the limitations of the lighter materials outweighed their advantages.

Tentmaking uses a lot of time and money. Since most of us have a finite amount of both, it makes sense to spend a little extra time and money for a lot of extra durability. In the long run, you'll be happier with your tent.

Working with non-tentage fabrics

If you're one of those brave souls who feel that you know enough about fabrics to be able to use less expensive material than the tentage fabrics, there are a few things you have to do to make it useable. First, you have to wash it to pre-shrink it and get the sizing out of it. This step may be skipped if you are using synthetic materials, but you may wish to test-wash swatches of natural/synthetic blends to see if shrinking occurs.

You don't need to physically stuff the entire roll in the washing machine. Instead, hang large pieces of it out on a clothesline, or drape it over a hedge, or otherwise get it off the ground. Then hose it down thoroughly and get it sopping wet. Let dry. Repeat until either the cloth stops shrinking or you run out of patience.

When I'm using cloth that I know isn't pre-shrunk, I've found it helpful to make two marks a known distance apart along the selvage with an indelible marker, and then shrink the cloth. That will give you a better indication of how much cloth you're actually going to need for your tent.

Another benefit of wetting the cloth down thoroughly and then allowing it to dry is that you wash all of the sizing out of the cloth and can then more accurately assess how the cloth will perform as a tent. There are a lot of cloths out there that change dramatically for the worse once all that stuff goes away, as people have found to their regret. This goes double for "mystery fabric" that people find at flea markets, garage sales, or remnant sales.

Remember that depending on the design of your tent, you might need to worry more about stretch than shrinkage. Most tents, after all, are tension structures. If the tents has a rigid frame or lots of side poles, the fabric isn't under much load and is more apt to shrink than stretch, but center-pole and hoop structures, conical tents, and sunshades are more affected by stretch.

A few other questions were asked about ascertaining the qualities of "mystery cloths" ... in particular, their ability to shed water. Checking to see if the fabric sheds water by beading tells you something, but if the material was originally sold as drop-cloths for painting, I would be concerned about how the water repellency was achieved, and whether the fabric's flammability was increased. I've seen drop-cloths that were oil-impregnated to help keep dust down and keep moisture from damaging them. I'd bet they would repel water marvelously. I'd also bet that they'd burn like candles, and would carefully flame-test a swatch of it before I started cutting it up into tent panels.

In fact, I'd flame-test it as a matter of routine. Even if it hasn't been treated for flame retardance, the composition of the cloth greatly affects its flammability. All untreated natural cloth tends to smolder and burn at a lower rate, whereas synthetic cloth often goes up with horrifying speed. I think I might also ask myself if any of the stuff used to finish the cloth might start out-gassing once the warm sun hits my tent, and whether I'd want to be breathing that stuff. The finishers of cloth made for tentage have presumably thought about that (at least, I'm sure their lawyers have). The finishers of your cloth might not.

While we're on the subject of materials, you must decide at this point whether you're going to paint it. Generally speaking, once a material is weatherproofed, it doesn't take paint well. (Sunforger is an exception.) So painting must take place before the weatherproofing. Also, as a rule, synthetic fabrics do not accept paint, although some silk-screen enamels work with some fabric. Awning fabrics with an acrylic finish will accept artist's acrylic paints. Synthetics also do not weatherproof well, and usually must be purchased already treated for that.

Your cloth should ideally be 6-ounce or more (that's the weight of a piece one yard square), although weights of as low as 3.5-ounce can be used if you are careful with reinforcements. If you use a material lighter than 6-ounce, reinforce the hems with ribbon or webbing, and your tent till last twice as long.

By the way, don't put too much faith on the accuracy of cloth weights. Some cloths are typed on their weight before additional fabric treatment is applied, others afterwards. Some weights are based on a sample of cloth that's 36" by 36" (a true square yard), while others on a dimension of 36" by 28 ½" (the old "clothyard" measure – or, to be more accurate, one of several old clothyard measures). Most civilized countries have gone to a measurement of grams per square meter, but American textile makers haven't caught up yet.

One question I am inevitably asked in my lectures is "Where can I get fabric?" The answer varies so much from one part of the country to the other that I can give you only a few guidelines. First, look around for fabric discounters that buy "odd lots" from mills. These are either first-quality overruns or second-quality cloths with color or finish flaws. The one I use most is ITEX in Colorado (phone 800-525-7058). One drawback is that they sell only full rolls (usually, but not always, 80 yards or more), so you might want to join forces with another person and combine your orders. Their stock changes from month to month, so call them for a current list. Other sources that sell only full rolls are periodfabric.com, Astrup, And Top Value Fabrics (and, depending on which sales representative you talk to, you might need a resale license). For Sunforger and other canvases sold by the yard, try Panther Primitives or Hamilton Dry Goods (http://hamiltondrygoods.com), but expect to pay a lot more. I'm told that all these companies have excellent customer service. But be careful to ask whether you're getting first-quality or second-quality stuff, If it's second-quality, you also need to know why it was downgraded. The reason might be something that you can work around, such as uneven width or selvedge, or in might be that the fabric treatment didn't adhere properly or left discolorations on the cloth.

When shopping for cloth, ask about shipping charges, and see if the cloth can be "drop shipped" to you from the mill. This might save a bundle in shipping charges, which can be steep if you don't live close to your vendor. Also, ask at your local awning shops or boat-cover makers if they have any excess cloth (left over from completed or cancelled jobs) that they'll sell you at cost.

14. Patches, Hems, and Seams

The mechanics of putting cloth together

If cloth was of exactly the right size for your use, and if it had infinite strength and manageable stretch over its entire width, there would be no point to this chapter, and I'd have to think of something else to write about. Fortunately for me, the world of cloth isn't that perfect, and even if it was, the fabric we'd see wouldn't look enough like period fabric to suit us re-creationists. So sew we must.

When you sew, use thread that matches your fabric, both in weight and material. Different materials have different hardnesses; mismatching them will eventually result in either the thread sawing through the fabric or vice versa. I'll discuss this in more detail in Chapter 15.

Every design is a compromise between weight and strength. We want to use the lightest cloth possible, to have less weight to carry around, less load on our various methods of transportation, and less strain on the tent's frame. But since lighter cloth is more susceptible to tears, abrasion, and stretching, we can't use it "off the roll" without reinforcing the areas that need it most.

Tears, abrasions, and stretching are the big three tent-killers. Tears happen either because the fabric suddenly sees a lot more strain than it usually does, and more than it's designed to take. This strain could be due to something else on the tent failing dramatically (like a pole or a rope) and transferring more of the normal stresses of a tent onto the hapless fabric, or it could be caused by point-loading --- the familiar tent pole (or lance-head) going through the fabric where it isn't supposed to.

To guard against these things, reinforcement must be provided. Like most people with backgrounds in sailmaking, I call these reinforcements "patches" even though, strictly speaking, they don't "patch" or repair anything. We use them to beef up those areas where we expect to see more stress than the fabric alone could handle.

Patches

Patches can be single layers of cloth or multiple layers. When using multiple layers (or very heavy cloth), care must be taken not to go from a thin area to a very thick area. Such a sharp transition will ensure that the border of the patch will flex more than the usual area, and flexion eventually results in the cloth weakening. It's exactly the same as bending that coat hanger wire back and forth to break it, although the weakening takes place over a much longer period of time. And if the area is shock-loaded, I'd bet dollars to donuts that the fabric will fail right at the transition area where the thick cloth, stretching not at all, passes all the stress it encounters on to the adjacent thin layer.

Look at the corner of a yacht sail. You'll see many layers of cloth at the grommet or Inox ring or whatever is used to attach the sail to the rest of the boat. Then you'll see the layers disappear, one by one, as you travel outward from the grommet. On a well-made tent, you're likely to see a similar system at major attachment points like the roof peak, where the grommet goes through the tent fabric, plus a layer or two of cloth on top of the tent fabric, to many layers (or webbing) at the peak itself.

When you sew patches to the cloth, try not to run the stitch lines at 90 degrees to the angle of greatest tension. Running a stitch line this way is bad because it loads the line at a point where it is weakest, and where any stress on the fabric will result in the thread "combing out" the fabric, reducing its integrity even more. Instead, try to run the seam lines parallel to the tension lines, or at least not much above 45 degrees from parallel.

What to use for patches? Most people use more of the cloth the tent is made of. In most cases, that works fine, and the patch material will probably stretch and age like the main fabric, too. You might eventually reach a thickness where your sewing machine has trouble going through all that stuff, but those areas can usually be hand-seamed with strong thread and a stout needle. Sailmakers use a "palm" -- a sort of fingerless glove with a concave surface on the palm, dimpled like a thimble, so they can use the force of their wrists and arms to drive the needle through. These doodads are hard to find, but your local awning shop, leather emporium, or sail loft can find you a source for them, and they're definitely worth the trouble to locate. They come, unsurprisingly, in left-hand and right-hand flavors. There's more about them in the "Tools" chapter.

You can also use leather (eight-ounce leather works well), although with leather patches you have to pay more attention to keeping the leather oiled and reasonably supple. If the leather gets dry and hard, it not only becomes crumbly and brittle, but it also creates, at its border, the going-from-stiff-to-soft transition I described earlier.

At really high-stress areas, where center poles are going through the fabric, I use webbing a lot. It's relatively low-maintenance, extremely strong, and usually used in areas where it isn't too visible.

Seams and Hems

The best type of seam to use is a flat-fell seam. These seams are made by overlapping the edges, with the "outsides" of the panel (or the "right" side, for you sewpeople) against each other. The lower edge protrudes from the upper panel about 1/2" to 1" as shown in Figure 31-A. You then sew a line of stitching that same distance (or a little more) from the edge of the upper panel, as indicated by the dotted line in Figure 31-A. The protrusion is then folded to the stitch line, as shown in 31-B. Figure 31-C shows how the panels are folded back with the sewn edge folded so that the protrusion ends up inside the seam. To finish the seam, sew another line of stitching sewn to hold the flap down, as shown in Figure 31-D. This method results in a strong, weathertight seam with all the cut edges concealed.

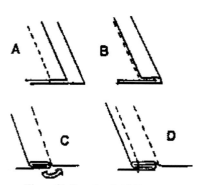

Figure 31. Forming flat fell seams

Try to avoid seaming horizontally. If you can't avoid it (for instance, when attaching a valance to a canopy, arrange it so that the outside fold is lapped downward. When assembling the seam, put the lower panel on the bottom, wrong side down, and put the upper panel on top, wrong side up. It's the lower panel that provides the seam's protrusion. If you did it right, there will be only a single stitch line showing on the outside. If you're confused by this explanation, practice with some scrap fabric.

The best tents are made with the seams oriented along the lines of the greatest tension. The Tentmasters company calls this technique "seam engineering," but the technique has been used by sailmakers and tentmakers for centuries. By orienting the seams this way, the seams themselves can act as reinforcements, the extra layers of cloth acting to limit the stretch along those lines. In fact, sailmakers often create a "false seam" simply by pinching the cloth to form an overlap and then sewing the overlap down. The resulting seam looks like, and performs like, a true seam, although there is only one piece of cloth involved. If your finished wall (or awning, or whatever) ends up being a couple of inches too wide, you can also use false seams to shorten it without needing to cut the fabric.

If the seam alone might not provide enough strength, you can make it stronger if you "rope" the seams by running a length of rope or webbing through the pocket formed inside the seams. The rope or webbing is usually sewn to the fabric along its entire length, although in some special applications, the rope is only sewn down at the ends. You'd use the latter technique where you feel you might have to replace the rope from time to time, or where you might want to adjust the rope's length to compensate for any stretching or shrinking of the fabric. The need for this compensation actually illustrates the main drawback of roping a seam -- it may make the seam stronger, but it doesn't do much to control stretch in the areas near the seam. And if stretch occurs, usually due to extreme wind loads on the tent, there may not be enough tension on the fabric to remove the bagginess. The result is a tent that luffs in the wind, and no amount of tension on the canopy will remove the bagginess until the rope inside the seam is loosened and retied at the point where the canopy is taking some of the strain again.

The trickiest seam to sew is one where the fabric has been cut on the bias – that is, the fabric has been cut diagonally from, instead of parallel with, either the warp (the threads that run the length of the bolt of the fabric) or the fill or weft (the threads that run the width of the bolt). These seams are troublesome because they stretch more, creating bagginess where you don't want it. Generally, if the cut is more less than fifteen degrees from the warp or fill, the stretch isn't enough to worry about, but for greater angles, you have to compensate somehow.

One way is to curve the seam. You do this by first making your cut along the panel (or at least marking where the cut will go). Then you draw a shallow arc along that same cut. I do this by driving a spike into my worktable at each end of the panel, and laying a long, flexible piece of molding (available from builders supply places) along the cut so that each end of the molding is stopped by the nail. Then I push inward at the center of the molding until I get the arc that I want, and secure the molding at that point with another spike. Finally, you draw the arc on the panel and trim along the line. If you don't have a work table that you don't mind driving nails or spikes into, you can achieve the same thing with a few helpers.

How much arc? That depends on the type and weave of the material and the stress that the seam is likely to encounter and, unfortunately, you won't know for sure until the tent is finished and erected. (This is where the professional tentmakers have an advantage, for they've been able to tweak their patterns over the course of time until they're satisfied. You don't have that luxury.) But as a rule of thumb, I'd go with at least one 1/2" per foot of seam. Yeah, that sounds like a lot, but it's better to overshoot than undershoot, since once the tension on the seam achieves a certain point, the roof curvature changes to accommodate it.

You can also control stretch to some extent by the aforementioned "roping" technique, using either rope or webbing sewn into or onto the seam. But this seldom works by itself, and is used only in conjunction with curving the seam.

Yet another way to control stretch is by sewing the bias-cut edge to another edge that runs along the warp or fill of the fabric. But you have to be careful here, because sometimes the adjacent area will stretch even if the seam itself doesn't. This is more pronounced on softer garment cloth than on the heavier tent cloth, which is why garment designers generally avoid this type of seam. But it has its place, particularly where the loads aren't great. For an example, read Appendix B, where I describe sewing the flap of the sunshade to the main body.

There's one place where many seams converge to a central point, and that's at the peak of the tent. If you're sewing a square tent, it's usually not too hard to manage the extra thicknesses, although you will have less to manage if you've thought to design the roof so that there's no seam running directly up the center of each roof side.

But if you're sewing a round tent, there's only one way to avoid having all your seams overlap at the peak, and that's by having all of them stop short of the peak. This means, of course, having a separate roof cone, with only one side seam, to which you sew your truncated roof panels. This gives you some other options, as well. You can choose to have the roof cone made of a heavier material, or a material of a different color.

One drawback of a roof cone is that as it wraps around the peak of the tent, it presents a different bias angle at each roof panel. There are places where the warp or weft of the cloth is parallel to that of the roof panel, but further along, there's puckering and stretching because the roof panel meets the cone panel where the threads are at 45° to each other. My solution to this problem kills two birds with one stone: I make two roof cones, laying them out and sewing them together with the warps laid out at 45° to each other. This doubles the cloth, resulting in greater strength at the peak, and also arranges things so that wherever a roof panel meets the cone at that 45° bias to one layer of the cone, it's in parallel with the warp or weft of the other layer, resulting in no pucker.

A hem is a sort of specialized seam at the edge of the cloth, but it serves the same function of providing more cloth where tension loads are greater. Of course, they also serve to finish the edge of the cloth so it doesn't unravel, but that's a secondary benefit. Even when I'm using the selvage of a cloth like Sunforger, I fold it over to form a hem, because even if it doesn't unravel, the edges of the cloth are going to get a lot of strain and more abrasion, and the selvage isn't really much different in composition than the rest of the cloth ... a little more tightly woven, it is true, but not enough to strengthen it appreciably.

Awning cloths like Pyrotone need hemming, because they don't have a true woven selvage. Instead, the cloth is simply trimmed to size, and it's the acrylic finish on the coat that keeps it from fraying for a little while. But fray it will, sooner or later. Similarly, urethane-coated nylons will resist fraying at first, but will eventually fray. (But you're not using nylon for tent material, are you?) And rest assured that heat-sealing any of these cloths will not keep them from fraying for long, regardless of what anybody tells you.

On my sunshades, there's a four-foot length at the bottom of each flap that is cut slightly on the bias of the cloth. The angle of the cut is enough to cause the flap to stretch and distort, so I prevent that problem by cutting two strips of fabric, 2" wide, on the fill (or weft) of the cloth and sewing that strip into the seam of the hem. I guess you could call the strip a sort of "anti-bias" tape. (I'm telling you this because there's no way of knowing, just by looking, that the strip was inside the seam, but it's attention to little details like this that make the difference in the way a tent looks and works.)

There's one last way to keep your tent fabric from stretching and distorting along the seams, particularly the roof, and that's by relieving the stress on the cloth in the first place. If the stress is due to the weight of a heavy ring or spokes supporting a round tent without side poles, ropes can be strung inside the tent from the ring (or spoke ends) up to a point on the center pole just below the top of the pole, so the rope doesn't touch the fabric itself. The rope length is then adjusted so it carries much of the weight of the frame and sidewalls, while leaving enough to keep the roof tensioned and free of sags or wrinkles. I've seen some very large tents that used this set-up effectively, and quite a few more that could have used it, but didn't. The owners of the latter tents eventually paid the price when the tents failed long before they should have.

15. The Right Machine and Workspace

Many people start making tents but get discouraged when they get the job underway and find themselves struggling. Over the years, I've learned a few tricks about how to make the project to go easier. Much of the trouble goes away when you have tools and workspaces that work for you instead of against you, and that's what this chapter is all about.

Sewing Machines and tables

The basic sewing tool nowadays is the sewing machine, which is the main reason that period tents are available at reasonable prices. Otherwise, the cost of labor would make them prohibitive to all but a very few.

One of the most common questions I get in my tentmaking classes is "What sort of sewing machine should I use?" The answer is that any sewing machine will work, as long as it's rugged enough. An industrial machine is the obvious first choice, especially if it's fitted with some sort of mechanism for feeding the material through the needle area. These machines are designed to run 24/7 if they need to, with a minimum of maintenance. Although they are pricy, they can be rented by the day or week around most metropolitan areas; call the various sewing machine suppliers in your area to see if they provide that service.

The key to whether a home machine can do the job is mostly a question of gears ... specifically, whether they're made of metal or plastic. Most of the older machines (prior to around 1970, I'd say) used metal gears and could be subjected to a lot more abuse without breaking. My friend Steve Peck likes to tell about how he tore up the plastic gears on his machine, but found when he took it in for repair that these gears could be replaced with metal ones. He had this done, and this machine is the one he uses for all of his heavy sewing nowadays.

Another factor is how powerful the motor is, and how efficiently the feed dog works in moving the material through the machine. This doesn't affect the quality of the stitches very much if you sew very carefully, but it affects the speed at which you are able to sew a seam. The weaker machines require a lot more attention in regulating the pace of the sewing and feeding the material through the machine.

A third factor is how heavily the presser foot presses on the work. This isn't strictly a matter of the compression of the presser spring alone, but is a combination of several factors, such as the thickness and weave of the canvas, the diameter of the needle, and the size of the thread. All these factors conspire to grab the needle and hold on to it as it passes through the fabric; when the needle goes up, the canvas wants to follow it. The presser foot's job is to keep that from happening, but the greater the friction on the needle, the harder that job is. One way to determine if this is going to be a problem is by trying to sew some canvas.

Here's a way to make a rough test of this. First, remove the thread from the needle and, without putting fabric through the machine, run it for a little bit. As it's running, put your finger on the presser foot. *Not under the needle, of course!* But you should be able to touch a part of the foot that's not in the needle's way. You'll get a sense of how much the presser foot moves up and down as it's being pushed by the feed dog.

Next, thread the needle and repeat the process, sewing multiple layers of cloth. Again, feel how much the presser foot wants to go up and down. If the foot's pressure can't handle the friction, you'll be able to feel the foot lifting slightly each time the needle goes up, as it attempts to drag the cloth along with it. That's bad news.

You might be able to compensate for this by increasing the foot pressure as described in the manual for your machine, but if it's a home machine there may simply not be enough of a range of adjustment. If there's a heavier spring available for your sewing machine, your dealer or repair person may be able to retrofit it; if not, you'd better look at another machine.

I'm told that there are some "slant-needle" machines, made for home sewing, where the needle isn't perpendicular to the sewing table. These machines aren't very good for sewing heavy material, as the needle experiences side loads it isn't engineered to take and subsequently bends and breaks.

Feeding mechanisms

Sewing machine motors, no matter how powerful they are, can use all the help they can get, and canvas workers have devised a variety of mechanisms to help get the fabric through the machine. The three most commonly used mechanisms are the walking foot, the puller, and the gravity ramp.

The walking foot pinches the cloth against the feed dog and moves with it, instead of just applying pressure against the feed dog and counting on the dog's traction to move the fabric along.

Most of the industrial machines made specifically to handle canvas and leather use such a mechanism. My main machine happens to be a Pfaff 545 with a walking foot, although I've used well-made walking-foot machines from Japanese manufacturers like Juki, Consew, and Brother.

Many of these Japanese manufacturers designed their machines to use parts in common, which increases the odds that your repair person will have the proper replacement part in stock at a reasonable price. (But when it comes to parts for industrial machines, your idea of a reasonable price may not agree with the manufacturer's.)

To be frank, I haven't seen an aftermarket walking-foot arrangement that works well for our purposes. They're designed to make it easier to sew gossamer fabrics without bunching it up under the pressure of the foot, but they don't add any additional ability to move heavy fabric through the machine.

The puller is a gadget seen most often on sailmaking machines, notably those made by Bernina (although I've seen a few Berninas and other models retro-fitted with them by California sewing-machine suppliers). It consists of a roller, behind the machine's foot, which is powered by the sewing machine's drive train. This roller is either above the table surface and presses the material against a smooth plate as it rotates, or is mostly under the table surface and pinches the cloth between itself and another roller, mounted over the fabric and pressing downward on it.

In the conventional setup, the foot is first engaged, as in a regular sewing machine. Then, if desired, the puller's moveable roller is lowered onto the work and the puller

Figure 32. Machine with Puller

becomes the primary mechanism for feeding the cloth. The roller is powered by the same linkage that drives the feed dog, and is adjusted so that it feeds the cloth through just a tad faster than the feed dog operates. Sailmakers prefer this system because it allows them to use a wider foot that accommodates the large zig-zag stitches that they use on sails. ("Why zig-zag?" I hear you ask. Because that seam will stretch with the fabric, eliminating the aerodynamically undesirable tension or "pucker" line that would otherwise result from the sailcloth stretching faster than the seam line.)

I have owned two puller-equipped Bernina 217s, one with a very slick puller setup from the factory and the other one with a retrofitted puller. They were bought primarily for the sail work I did, although they were occasionally used for straight-seaming work. The big trouble with Berninas is that the parts are expensive. As a sewing machine dealer told me, "The Bernina is the Porsche of industrial sewing machines, and you've got to expect to pay Porsche prices."

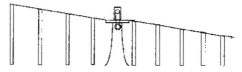

Figure 33. A gravity-feed ramp

The third system, also used by sailmakers, is the gravity ramp. As the name suggests, it's simply an inclined ramp that feeds the cloth through the machine. It's by far the cheapest system, and sailmakers claim that it's the easiest to regulate, since gravity doesn't change much from day to day. Seen from the side, it looks like Figure 33.

I remember the slope as being roughly 7 or 8 degrees in one of the lofts I worked in, but it isn't critical. The ramp should be about the length of the longest seam you commonly sew, usually seven or eight feet (although longer seams can be sewn if you fold the work accordian-style and have a helper around to refold the work as it hits the bottom of the lower ramp). The most awkward part of using a gravity ramp is muscling the cloth back up the ramp when you have to backstitch, but sailmakers don't usually do much of that.

The gravity-feed system can easily be improvised from whatever four-by-eight paneling you may have available ... plywood, particle board, Masonite, or paneling. Since it doesn't have to be pretty or even full-width, it's worth asking your local purveyors of such stuff whether they have any damaged, cracked, scratched, scuffed, or otherwise discountable panels in their stock that they'd be willing to part with at their cost or a little over. All you need to make it serviceable is a little paste wax to let the fabric slide down the ramp a little easier. At the loft, we finished it with a urethane varnish, waxed it with floor wax, and kept it touched up with a silicone spray to keep it slippery.

The sewing table

At my most recent shop, my sewing table was twenty-four feet long and twelve feet wide, with the sewing machine installed halfway along one of the long sides. This gave me twelve feet in front of the machine, twelve in back, and twelve on the side ... enough to spread out large sections of material. You probably don't need anything quite that big, but you should have enough to be able to support the length of a panel seam front and back. If your sidewalls are six or seven feet high, two pieces of 4' x 8' paneling, plywood, or whatever will make a decent front-and-back table when supported by sawhorses so that the paneling is the height of your sewing table. The advantage of this system is that you can easily configure it into an 8' x 8' cutting table, move it around indoors or outdoors, and break the whole thing down for easy storage when it isn't in use. Laid on top of sawhorses of varying leg lengths, they can also serve as a gravity ramp.

Sky hooks

Well, they're not really used to hang things from the sky, but I like the term. The one illustrated at right is a variation of what I saw parachute makers do at the Pioneer Parachute Company, where I did some production engineering in the early 1980's. Their seamstresses had to sew the skirts of, and attach lines to, the huge parachutes used by the military to drop heavy equipment. They solved the problem of handling

Figure 34. A "sky hook" in use

the massive amounts of material by hanging the parachute from the ceiling by its peak, with the skirt right at the level of the sewing machine. The suspension system carried the whole weight of the cloth, so the operators only needed to maneuver the adjacent part of the parachute through the machine. If your sewing area has a high ceiling (about twelve feet or so), you may be able to use this system when sewing the bottom of the canopy of the tent, as shown in Figure 34.

A pulley is attached to the ceiling, and a rope is fed through it. One end of the rope has a C-clamp and a carabiner on it, and the material to be sewn is attached to the pulley either by a loop fed through the hole in the roof's peak and clipped to the carabiner (if the work piece has a hole there) or by being clamped with the C-clamp (if it doesn't). If the material is clamped, the

107

clamp should be well padded so that the work piece's fabric isn't crushed. The work piece is then raised to the appropriate level, and other end of the rope is attached to a cleat on the table, allowing the work piece to hang at the right height.

Needles and thread

The right needle, as Goldilocks might say, is one that's not too big and not too small. The people who sell you the thread should be able to make the best recommendation, or direct you to the manufacturers of the thread or the needles. Or you could experiment with an assortment, starting on scrap with the larger ones and going down a size at a time until you start having problems. Later on in the chapter, I'll give some more specific recommendations to get you started.

Your present sewing machine needles are probably too small to sew canvas, and that's not good. Sewing canvas creates a lot of friction, friction creates heat, and smaller needles don't do as good a job of dissipating heat as the larger ones do. Therefore, they overheat and lose their temper, which makes them flex weirdly, miss stitches, and maybe even shatter or plunge into the hook or worse, making you lose *your* temper. Also, smaller needles have smaller eyes, and running a heavy thread through a small eye can throw off thread tensions and affect the ability of the top thread to form a loop big enough for the hook to catch as it rotates.

The temptation is often to be on the safe side and use a larger needle than you need. That's better than going too small, but it's not an ideal solution. Since you are poking a hole into the material with every stitch, and bigger holes make it easier for moisture to seep through the tent roof, it stands to reason that you don't want to make holes too big.

There are two schools of opinion about the proper needle point. Some manufacturers use only "ball end" needles, on the theory that the needle will be less likely to cut the fibers of the material. Others (myself included) feel that this theory works better for sewing done at a relatively slower rate, but that for a machine running fast or powerfully, a sharp needle will be less likely to damage the material, since it is better able to push the fibers aside rather than crush them with blunt force. It really doesn't matter much. Use the ones that give you the best result, or can obtain the cheapest.

How often do you change a needle? I change it when it starts screwing up. As experienced sewers know, it will eventually get to the point where you can sense it by a slight increase in noise or effort from the sewing machine. When I was running a six-machine sail loft, I could often hear a dull needle from across the room! But there are other indications, too. If you use an industrial machine that uses needles without a flat side, you can check the straightness by rolling it along the table and seeing if the point "wobbles." Or examine the point of the needle with a magnifying glass. If you can see a glint of light anywhere on the point, the point has a flat spot and has to be replaced. But lots of times, you just can't tell visually when a needle is due to be replaced. My advice: when the machine starts to drop stitches or otherwise misbehave, first replace the needle, and see if the fresh needle makes your sewing easier. Nine times out of ten, that fixes the problem. If it doesn't, there probably was still some life left in the old needle, and the solution is to find out what else is wrong with the machine.

Sometimes it's the thread itself. If the thread resists going through the needle's eye or through many thicknesses of fabric and protests by looping on the underside, here's an old sailmaker's trick: take the top thread spool and spray it well with a silicon spray lubricant, let it sit, and spray it again. Then put it in a baggie and let it sit overnight. Repeat as necessary. (Or immerse the thread overnight in a coffee can with liquid silicon lubricant.) This trick works wonders with any tough sewing job, such as capes or leatherwork.

You could also try switching your top and bottom thread spools. The top thread has to be of higher quality than the bottom (bobbin) thread, because it works harder. It has to be more flexible as it wends its convoluted way through the various guides and tensioning mechanisms. And it also has to deal with the alternating slack and tension inflicted by the tensioning arm (sometimes called the lever arm, take-up arm, or the Thing That Goes Up And Down). Compared with the workout that the top thread gets, the bottom thread really has life easy. So you can usually put your cheaper, stiffer thread on the bottom without ill effect.

Speaking of thread, the people who sold you the fabric will probably have some recommendations. I prefer a bonded polyester "anti-wick" thread since I haven't seen a cotton thread that will match it for strength and durability. Cotton threads are weaker and more prone to weather damage, but have the advantage of swelling slightly when wet and sealing the seam. You generally want to match the thread to the fabric, material-wise, although I've had good luck sewing all-cotton material with all-polyester thread. I wouldn't recommend sewing synthetic materials with cotton thread, though, since it's a drag to have the seaming thread wear out before the material itself does. Sewing seams once is a real trial, but who wants to do it twice?

When you start talking about needle sizes and thread sizes with your salesperson, be sure you're using the same standards.

Here's a table that gives the needle sizes used in most canvas sewing:

US Size	Metric Size
13	85
14	90
15	95
16	100
17	105
18	110
19	120
20	125
21	130
22	140
23	160

And here's another table, showing what needle and thread sizes are recommended for a given weight of fabric. It's referring to stranded (not monofilament) polyester thread:

Fabric Weight	TKT size	T285 Size	Textile Size	Needle Recommended
1 1/2 ounces or less	V-30	AA		#12 or #14
3 ounces or less	V-46	B	45	#14 or #16
6 ounces or less	V-69	E	70	#16 or #18
11 ounces or less	V-92	F	90	#18 or #20
over 11 ounces	V-138	FF	135	#20 or #22

Two comments are in order here. First, you'll find that very few home sewing machines are up to handling V-138 thread; practically speaking, V-92 is about as heavy as you can go, or even need to go. This size works fine with the commonly available 10.10 ounce Sunforger. Second, if you're going with a polyester thread, be sure to specify a bonded, non-wicking thread. The bonded part is important, because it means that the thread has been treated to be smoother, to go through the machine much more easily, and more consistent in finish, so it doesn't force you to keep re-adjusting the tension. For what it's worth, the stuff I use is Heminway & Bartlett's "Dabond 2000" Dacron thread, with the anti-wick finish. The little more it costs has paid for itself over the years in smoother production and greater peace of mind.

As for non-polyester threads, there's such a range available that my advice wouldn't be much good, but the Industrial Sewing Machine people of Molalla, Oregon have put a multitude of data on their web site, including several detailed charts of thread/needle match-ups. Their web site can be found at: (http://www.industrialsewmachine.com/webdoc3/thread.htm), and chances are that you'll find what you need there.

Any sewing machine has its limitations, even the strongest industrial machine. Take it slow, hand-cranking the machine when going through thick stuff. You'll probably have to do some hand stitching as well, with a thick needle and sewing palm.

When good machines go bad

Suppose you've done everything I recommended above and your machine is still skipping stitches or breaking needles or whatever. At this point, most people would seek out their sewing machine guru and put the job in his or her hands. But machine adjustment isn't rocket science, and if you're mechanically apt, there's a chance you can fix it yourself, or at least noodle out the problem so your guru has a head start on diagnosing and fixing the problem.

I'm not going to get into this in detail, because so much depends on your particular brand of machine. But the folks at Sailrite have put much valuable advice on their web site (http://www.sailrite.com/techindex.htm), including fairly clear explanations of how certain adjustments are made and why they're important. It's well worth a visit to their site. If you keep having the same problem over and over again, like your hook continually floating out of adjustment, ask your guru to show you the technique to re-align it, so you can do it yourself next time.

If your industrial machine seems to have only two speeds – on and off – it means that your clutch is shot. It's not an expensive rebuild, and you only need to do it every ten years or so, so it's worth the investment. If you're lucky, the clutch may simply need adjusting rather than rebuilding.

Before starting your sewing project, it helps to give the machine a good cleaning and oiling. Certainly, once it comes back from the shop, promise it that you'll be good to it and oil it without fail. And keep the promise!

16. Hand Tools

Once you've got your sewing machine, you've got the main piece of equipment you'll need. But you'll still need a basic kit of tools. Many of them you may already have, and others can be scrounged from friends, so your outlay of cash might not be as great as you fear.

Shears

This what we professional cloth-whackers call the items you call "scissors." I'll call them shears since that's what the suppliers call them, and it takes our discussion to a somewhat loftier plane. If you want to call them scissors, by all means do so.

The shears I use most are my trusty Wiss 10" knife-edge shears (#1225), which work equally well on cotton as on synthetic materials. They are available in a right-hand configuration only, which is fine with me, since I learned to cut with either hand. (In sailmaking, the patterns are laid out with the assumption that the cutter will be using right-handed shears, and lefties like me had to adapt.) If you're a southpaw through and through, Wiss makes a very similar pair of shears, their #20, which comes in a left-hand as well as a right-hand configuration.

The Marks company, another major supplier to the textile market, makes similar shears at similar prices. And there are other heavy-duty shears suitable for canvas, but I haven't tried them and therefore can't recommend them (but that's not saying that they won't do the job just fine.)

I keep the shears very sharp, so that I can cut the material by simply running the cloth through the slightly opened blades, rather than snipping them. This saves a lot of strain on the hands. Your local sewing center probably has a scissor-sharpening service where you take your shears and give them back to you a day or so later. If they do a good job (and many of them don't, so it might be worth looking around), the service is well worth the modest price they charge. In my shop there's a little gizmo called a "shear sharpener" which consists of a little vise to hold the shear blade and a sharpening stone that I can adjust to a specific angle. That device, and a fine Arkansas or diamond stone to give that final edge and touch it up between sharpenings, are all I use. These shear sharpeners aren't cheap, but they've paid for themselves over twenty years, not only in cost but in convenience. If I damage an edge, I can restore it in minutes and not put a snag in production.

The only other cutters you'll need are a pair of thread clips and a seam ripper. The ones in your sewing kit will work fine. My personal preference in thread clips is the Wiss TC1, because I can easily resharpen them with the same shear-sharpening setup described above.

If you've got access to a cutting room with cloth saws and fancy rotary cutters, knock yourself out, but there's no need for that stuff unless you're doing serious production.

Other sewing tools

There are times when you'll need to put a needle through more cloth than your sewing machine wants to take. For these times, you'll need a heavy hand—sewing needle and some method of getting it through the fabric. I use sailmakers needles made by William Smith Company, which have a triangular cross-section designed to penetrate canvas with ease, but any heavy needle will suffice.

To get the needle through the fabric, I use a sailmaker's palm, which is a glove-like contraption with a concave thimble built into the palm, allowing me to push the needle through the fabric with all the force my arm can muster. Other folks use pliers to push or pull the needle through the fabric, but pliers will eventually scratch the needle and increase its drag through the fabric. Palms can be had from sailmaker's

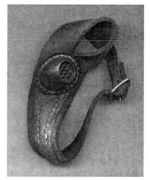

Figure 35. A sewing palm

suppliers or leathercraft suppliers (notably Tandy, which closed all its retail stores a few years ago, but recently repented its folly and reopened most of them). Palms are available in left-hand and right-hand configurations.

I've also got one of those "stitch awls" that have the bobbin built into the handle of the tool, but I've never found them very useful.

Grommet Setting Tools

Grommets (or eyelets, as they're called in British-speaking parts of the world) are metal fittings that are pressed into holes that you wish to reinforce. They are customarily used where

113

poles protrude through the fabric, and occasionally where stake loops or ties attach. But you knew that, right?

But you may not know that there are two main flavors of grommets. The ones that are stocked by most of the fabric stores and hardware stores are plain grommets, or sheet grommets. They're stamped from sheets (as you may have suspected) and are set with tools consisting of a flaring tool and a little anvil or die, which you can buy from the same people who sold you the grommets. They work fine for most purposes.

If the grommets take a lot of load, particularly sideways load, you might be better off the second flavor, which is the rolled-rim spur grommet. These have little teeth on the washer side to help anchor the washer more firmly into the fabric. Both the top and bottom pieces have edges that are "rolled over" instead of simply de-burred, which is a lot easier on the fabric itself. As you might expect, these grommets are more expensive than the first type, and so are the tools you need to set them ... and you can't use the plain-grommet tools on spur grommets, and vice versa.

About these tools: most of them are made by two companies, Osborne and Stimson. The Stimson tools are what the professionals use. They are made of harder steel, which makes them far more durable (although they tend to break more with ill use, the downside of hard, brittle steel). They also set more positively in thicker material (or more layers of material). And they cost more – a lot more, typically four or five times the cost of the Osborne tools. Over the years, I've compromised on the expenses, investing in Stimson tools for the #0 and #1 spur grommets, which are what I use the most. For the rest of the sizes I use (#000 to #5), the Osborne tools are good enough. I wouldn't invest in the Stimson tools unless you intend to make many, many tents.

If you have grommet tools, you must use a rawhide or plastic mallet with them. Using steel hammers will kill these tools.

Use this same mallet on the cutters that you employ to punch grommet holes in the canvas. These guys also come in two basic flavors: The "arch" hole cutter, where the part you pound on is in a direct line with the hole, and the "side" hole cutter, where this part is slightly offset. They work about the same, and cost about the same, so the difference isn't worth worrying about.

Lastly, you'll need a cutting pad for the cutter to cut into when it's finished cutting through the canvas. Sailmakers use a vinyl cutting-block about half an inch thick; the nylon can be cut into several times before it starts getting so chewed up that it crumbles, and the soft surface protects the edge of the tool. My preference is a piece of UHMW (short for "ultra high molecular weight") plastic that I picked up from a scrap seller, which does the same job but lasts far longer. If you want to go the absolute cheapest route, you can use scrap softwood (or softwood plywood) if you don't mind the splinters.

Fasteners

When you're seaming panels together, you need some method of attaching them so as to keep them in alignment as they go through the machine. The fasteners I use most are T-pins, staples, spring clips, and Seamstick.

T-pins come in various sizes (I generally use the 1 ½" ones) and work well if the material is soft, but don't work as well on canvas much heavier than ten ounces in weight. For this stuff, I use a Swingline plier stapler loaded with P22 staples. (This is basically the same stapler that you see at the checkout counters where they insist on stapling your bags shut.) I've modified mine by taking off the circular "guard" at the bottom of the grip so that the jaws are more parallel to the table. To remove these staples, I don't use those stupid little jaw-like staple removers. Instead, my weapon of choice is the Vise-grip 5" locking plier wrench. This gadget has the advantage of being able to remove staples regardless of whether, once the seam is folded, the part of the staple that's exposed is the top "bar" or the folded-over legs. If you can get the tool on any part of the staple that happens to be visible, the staple will come out without a whimper. (I remember coming to work at a sail loft where they used staples extensively, and all the workers had the little jaw-like removers. "This is very bogus," I thought, and went out to my car to retrieve my trusty little Vise-grips. Within a week or so, all the other sailmakers in the loft had purchased their own Vise-grips.)

Spring clips are those clips you get at the office supply store. I use them more to keep panels rolled up so they go through the machine more easily than to clamp the pieces together, but they have their uses for aligning pieces of cloth. If you use them this way, you'll need to use a lot of them to keep the cloth in alignment.

The last fastener I use is a double-sided tape called Seamstick, another article that sailmakers use extensively. It sticks well to many awning fabrics (but not very well to Sunforger or Sunbrella) and since you don't have to remove it afterwards, it saves some time. It also adds a little sealing to the seams. Its biggest asset is that it allows you to align the panels with great precision, and maintains that alignment as the material is being sewn.

Seamstick is expensive when you buy it by the roll. I buy it fifty rolls at a time, good for about twenty tents, so I pay a little less.

Rulers and measuring devices

I don't have much to say about these, since you've probably been using them since kindergarten. But I will admonish you not to trust them too much. There was a yardstick in my sail loft that caused me no end of grief until I held it up against another yardstick and found that it was one eighth of an inch shorter (and, no, it wasn't a wooden ruler but a metal one). It probably wouldn't have mattered much for tents, but it made a great deal of difference in hang glider sails, for reasons I'll explain shortly.

About the only trouble you can get into is if you measure one panel when it's stretched to a different tension than another, so try to keep your tensions as consistent as you can.

One thing you can do to reduce variation in measuring is to use patterns and try-sticks wherever possible. My most-used patterns are made of fourteen mil Mylar (or equivalent), but I've used cardboard with good result, and butcher paper with less good result. It really helps if the pattern material is thick enough to trace around without getting pushed aside by the pencil or whatever. Patterns also make a record of what you did, so if a seam looks bad on your finished tent, you can compensate on the next tent by tweaking the pattern.

Try-sticks are essentially single-purpose measuring rulers. They are intended to mark out one dimension only, which means that as long as you use the same try-stick to measure out the panels of a wall, all those panels will be the same length with no chance of mismeasurement. They are great for production. In my old fifteen-person sail loft, I went to great pains to design sail production using patterns and try-sticks as much as humanly possible, so that people would have no need of rulers at all.

Marking and layout tools

The most common marking tool, of course, is the pencil. The softer the lead, the more visible a mark it leaves, and the more often it must be resharpened. A harder lead (a #4, for example) will leave a thinner but fainter line, and are used extensively in sailmaking where the thickness of a pencil line can make a great deal of difference in the performance of a sail. (This is particularly true in aviation sailmaking, where you're actually making two sails, exact mirror images of each other, for the left wing and the right wing. If they differ the slightest bit, one wing will fly more inefficiently than the other, and the glider will have a built-in turn. But I digress...)

I used to treat carpenter's flat pencils with disdain, but some nifty sharpeners have appeared on the market that give these pencils a much sharper point. I still feel that the lead in these pencils is too soft for much of the work I do, but on fabrics that don't take a pencil line well, this is the pencil to use.

To err is human, and I must be as human as anybody, because I've tried just about every eraser on the market. The ones that work best are called "Magic Rub" erasers, and they're available from most office supply stores. They're reasonably cheap, do almost as well as well as art gum erasers without nearly the shedding, and last longer than the art gum jobs.

On dark material, it's hard to get an easily visible line with most pencils. I use white fabric markers, which I get from the John Boyle Company. They're only available in boxes of a hundred, but I love them.

I've had some experience with ball-point pens as well, and still use them where pencils won't work (such as laying out lines on the vinyl I use for ground cloths) but I'm not wild about them because the ink can smear and run, thereby disfiguring the work. If you feel that only a ball-point will do the job for you, I would recommend the "Write Brothers" pen, which seems to have the most durable writing tip of all the cheapo pens. With this brand, you run less risk of the pen point heating up with the friction of drawing a long line, disintegrating, and making a mess.

For marking webbing or other really rough material, I use the same tailor's chalk that you can buy at the fabric shop.

The other tools I use when laying out are a right-angle (your basic framing square), several straight-edges in lengths from six inches (roughly 150 mm) to eight feet (about two and a half meters) long, and a ten-foot (three meter) piece of quarter-round molding. This last piece is for generating smooth curves. After the points along the curve are plotted, the strip of moulding is laid along them and secured with push pins or scratch awls (described below) while the line is drawn onto the fabric or pattern.

For very long lines that must be absolutely straight, a chalk line is used ... the same tool that construction people use. Since the chalk tends to be messy, I use it mainly to lay out straight lines on patterns or working surfaces, lay down some thick tape along the line, and then transfer the line to the fabric by running a pencil down the fabric along the ridge that can be felt through the cloth.

Holding devices

When laying out the panels, I use sailmaker's push pins, which look a lot like the push pins you use on bulletin boards, but usually have a larger cap and a thinner, sharper shank. I've also used staples applied with an ordinary staple gun.

If I need to keep the cloth attached to the table even if I'm pulling on it with vigor, I also use "scratch awls" (sometimes also called "spikes" in the sailmaking biz but not to be confused with the "wire spikes" you make tent stakes from). These awls look just like the ones you use to put holes in leather and such, except that their points are thinner and sharper, and they're made of stronger steel.

Cloth Wrangling

One thing that makes rolling out cloth much easier is some sort of rack, such as the one pictured at the right. It can be either portable or mounted onto the table, like the one shown. It

Figure 36. A dispensing cloth rack

allows you to pull fabric directly off the roll and onto your cutting table. Believe me, it saves a lot of effort in picking up heavy rolls of cloth, turning them around, and trying to keep the fabric clean. The one pictured is home-built, with a long two-by-four at the base, two shorter uprights with notches cut in the top, and a long broom handle. There's a headless nail driven into the notch of one of the uprights that engages with a hole drilled into the broom handle. The nail keeps the broom handle from moving side to side and falling out of the notches.

To keep stuff rolled up or otherwise organized, I use spring clips and "Pony" type spring clamps, just like the ones you get at the hardware store.

Other doodads

When cutting synthetic cord, I use a hot knife (actually two of them, one like a soldering iron with a flat blade, the other like a soldering gun.) The work is put on a piece of glass, from which the melted gunk is occasionally scraped with a used utility knife blade. The flat-bladed hot knife is also useful for heat-sealing synthetic fabrics, but don't assume that this seal is permanent. I've seen too many of these edges fray over time to believe it. It's used mainly for controlling fray before the edge is concealed by being sewn into a seam or hem.

I don't use utility knives much, preferring a sharp pair of shears, but others find them useful.

Another tool some folks like to use is an iron for pressing seams prior to sewing.

If you've ever tried to roll up a twenty-foot length of soft cloth lengthwise all by yourself, you know how incredibly difficult that can be. I solved this problem by taping together a bunch of the cardboard tubes that fabric is commonly rolled on. It's relatively easy to roll the fabric around the tube and then slide the tube out of the end of the roll.

17. Fabric Treatments

This chapter is mainly for those who have, against my good advice, insisted on using cloth for their tents that wasn't designed for tentage. Their tents work well in fair weather, but when the weather turns foul and rainy the shortcomings of the non-treated fabric become all too apparent. It may also be that the tent was indeed made of water-repellent fabric, but that whatever treatment that was originally applied has long since given up the spirit. (Often, tents that have been aggressively treated for mildew lose much of their water-repellent finish and require re-treatment.) And there is the occasional temporary need to have a tent that's flame-retardant, for venues where that requirement is strictly enforced. All this is covered in the following chapter.

Waterproofing

From time to time, people ask me how to waterproof their canvas tents, usually after an event where it rained really, really hard. My answer has been one that they didn't want to hear, which is that the ideal waterproofing compound does not exist. But there are products on the market that help.

I know of three types of waterproofing compounds that have been used with varying rates of success. The first are silicone-based treatments, which are sprayed onto the cloth until some saturation is achieved. You buy it in liquid form, which you apply full strength with a garden sprayer (which, needless to say, you buy new and dedicate to the sole function spraying waterproofing and not Roundup or insecticides). It is also available, at much greater cost, in an aerosol can; one variety is called "Camp Dry" and is made by Kiwi (yes, the shoe polish people) and distributed through chains like K mart. These silicone-based treatments are essentially industrial-strength versions of "Scotch-Gard." Rather than filling the pores in the fabric, they deposit a layer of silicone that prevents the moisture from getting a grip on the cloth. They have a slight but distinct kerosene-like odor when applied, which mostly disappears with time and ventilation. Since the stuff doesn't saturate the threads of the fabric, it probably doesn't do much damage to the fire-retardant properties of the cloth or its ability to "breathe" (that is, allow water vapor to pass through the cloth). Its downside is that it doesn't do as good a job of waterproofing as the other compounds, is expensive, and requires re-treatment about once a year.

The second class is wax-based sealants, of which the most popular flavor is Canvak (a trademark of Buckeye Fabric Finishing Co, Coshocton, Ohio). These fabric sealers are available from some tentmakers, some awning supply houses, and possibly other sporting goods stores. The stuff comes in liquid form, which you either brush on or spray on with a spray rig. It does provide a good watertight seal for canvas, but has drawbacks of its own:

- It adds a bit of weight and stiffness to your tent
- As it dries (and possibly afterwards) it gives off fumes that you may or may not be sensitive to.
- It destroys whatever fire-retardant properties the cloth might have had
- If the cloth breathed before the treatment, it probably won't afterwards.

The third compound is Thompson's Water Seal, which people have sworn by, at, and off for some time now. It has all the properties listed above, plus the additional one of possibly harming your fabric. The people who make Water Seal say that it's supposed to be used to seal wood and masonry and such, and specifically exclude fabric from their list of applications, causing me to wonder if they know something that we don't (if you doubt me, you can read their disclaimers directly from the Thompson's web site at http://www.waterseal.com/).

One of the explanations for the varying results people have had with Water Seal may rest in the product's formulation. The story I've heard is that at some point, Thompson reformulated their product for the California market to comply with that state's "clean air" requirements. The formulation did significantly reduce the amount of noxious gases released into the atmosphere, but it also reduced the effectiveness of the compound as a fabric sealer. After a while, the story goes, they've started withdrawing the old formulation from other markets as well, so different people in different parts of the country are liable to get the new formulation instead of the old one.

Home-Brewed Waterproofing

If you've done research in the various books on camping, you will come across various concoctions for do-it-yourself waterproofing compounds. They usually involve procuring some old-fashioned laundry soap (the kind that came in brick-hard bars), dissolving it in hot water, and steeping the tent in the brew. After the tent is partially wrung out and dried, a second bath of hot water and alum is prepared, and the steeping process is repeated. Since alum is a fixative, this second step locks the remaining soap into the fabric. The problem with this sort of recipe is procuring the ingredients. The alum can be bought at art supply stores, but when you go shopping for the laundry soap, you might as well be asking for spats or buggy whips.

Other recipes involve dissolving paraffin (the wax used mostly in canning fruit) into white gas, benzene, or turpentine until maximum saturation is reached. Then you paint the tent with this mixture and let it dry until all the gasoline evaporates. Given what we know now about the toxic properties of these solvents, the recipes seem positively quaint. They were obviously the product of a more innocent age, but I value my lungs and nervous tissue too much to attempt to whip up some of this concoction and verify its efficacy.

I think this treatment was used on the tents we used in my Scouting days, which were surplus "shelter halves" from World War Two. If I recall, it had two drawbacks: it almost completely destroyed the breatheability of the canvas (not a problem for a shelter half, really), and when the material got really warm, like in the trunk of a car, the paraffin would tend to migrate, resulting in layers stuck together and generally uneven coverage.

Some people have reported success with ordinary latex exterior house paint. You thin it down with water and apply it to the canvas with a brush. Since latex paint varies wildly in its thickness and its proportion of binders (the part of the paint that provides the protective "skin") and solvent (the liquid that dries up and disappears), some experimenting with the ratio of paint to water is recommended. Find a few scraps of a canvas similar to your tent's fabric, and start with a one-to-one ratio. Let the scrap dry, and try to roll it up into a tube. Then scrunch it up into a ball. If the paint layer is too thick, it will make the canvas less flexible, and it might even crack. What you're trying to achieve is a layer of paint just thick enough to seal the fabric without adding too much stiffness

Latex paint is inexpensive and relatively safe to apply, but it may not adhere to a cloth that has any of its original waterproofing left. And it will probably have to be renewed periodically as the paint is exposed to sunlight and deteriorates. (In fact, that's what it's designed to do. See the chapter on painting your tent to discover why.)

For more information on waterproofing, first-hand experience, hearsay, and much confusion, you can read what others have posted on the Rialto and other Internet fora on the subject. Much of it is archived on the Internet at Tanya Guptill's *Medieval Pavilion Resources* or *Stefan's Florilegium*.

Flame Retardants

There seems to be some confusion about what sorts of flame retardants are used by companies for what purposes, so a few explanations are in order here.

California law requires that tents sold there be treated to a flame retardant standard called CPAI-84. This standard has two specifications, the first being that the material must be reluctant to burn or, more accurately, be unable to support the combustion process. To determine this, the material is ignited by a flame of a certain temperature. When this flame is removed, the fire should go out.

The second specification is that the treatment be good for the life of the fabric. It's this second specification that separates the CPAI-84 stuff from all the after-market treatments. Most of the latter are water-soluble and, when properly applied to the material, do a good job of retarding flame. For this reason, they are used on theater and sound-stage sets, hotel lobbies, and other areas where you want to keep fires from happening. But the treatment is not much good for tents, because tents get rained on, and the treatment dissolves and goes away.

There are six or seven other states in the United States that also require flame-retardant properties of tents that are made or sold there, but as far as I know, they all seem to be using California's CPAI-84 standards or a close variant. Other states and localities don't attempt to enforce a standard for camping tents, but local authorities may require flame-retardant properties for tents used in special venues like fairs.

If you don't use your tent much, but want to treat it for a specific purpose (such as use on a merchant's row where local ordinances mandate flame retardant treatment), you can treat the tent and just pray it doesn't rain. Depending on your locality, this may be a feasible strategy – in coastal California, for example, it usually stays dry from May to October, and other areas have such a scarcity of rain that the odds are good that you won't get rained on.

One aftermarket flame retardant is something called *Flameout*. This product comes in two flavors, one for basic fabric protection and one that resists stains as well. I'm not endorsing it, because I haven't tried it. But it may serve your purposes. Its manufacturer claims that the treatment is non-toxic and will even survive a couple of washings.

A typical formula for "home-made" fire retardant is one I found in an issue of Argent Advocate, published by Bjo Trimble for the SCA's Twenty-Five Year Celebration. (The article is uncredited, but presumably was written by her.) The formula and instructions, quoted verbatim, are:

1/2 cup ammonium phosphate
1 cup ammonium chloride
1 quart water
Check mix on scrap of tent fabric for color change. Spray or brush both sides of fabric w/mixture. Mix more as needed & continue to spray tent. Let dry. It's water-soluble; treatment should be repeated after exposure to rain.

Obtain chemicals at garden store, chemical supply or sometimes at drugstores.

Use normal precautions in mixing & handling: rubber gloves, mask when spraying, etc. Store fire retardant in glass or plastic (not metal) container.

KEEP OUT OF REACH OF CHILDREN & PETS!

18. Tent Poles

Most of the poles I've seen on the best tents have been made of wood, so most of this chapter will be devoted to that material. Indeed, some purists would scorn the use of anything but wood, but metal and plastic poles have their uses as well.

Wood

Wood species differ greatly in several properties. Some of these properties, like grain figure, nail-holding, and resistance to decay are not very important to their use as tent poles. But other properties, such as strength, stiffness, weight, and stability are crucial to their performance.

Strength and stiffness are not the same thing. Strength is a measure of the total load that the pole will take before it fails, whereas stiffness is a measure of its resistance to deflection. Since almost all of the load on a pole is compression, stiffness is given more importance than it might otherwise be accorded. We already know that if the pole is more than a diameter or so "out of column," its ability to withstand a load is seriously compromised. A stiffer pole will resist further bending. In the example of a tent pole, it's the measure of how much the pole will resist deflection if you lean on the middle of it when the tent is up.

Bending strength, on the other hand, measures how much load a piece of wood can bear if the two ends are supported and a weight is attached to the middle. In the case of our tent pole, it's how many pounds of lateral force the pole takes before it breaks. I don't consider that as important as stiffness, because once the pole deflects, it becomes more susceptible to failure than when it was straight. The figure for bending strength doesn't pre-suppose that the piece isn't already compression-loaded, although that's going to be the condition for any tent-pole under real-life loads. Moreover, by that time the tent has distorted and lost much of its ability to deflect wind loads, resulting in more of those loads getting transferred to the pole, which deflects it even more ... a cycle that only stops when the pole gives way, or when the tent finds another way to vent its load (e.g., pulling up tent stakes and collapsing).

But stiffness alone isn't the answer. I've seen oak poles, which are very stiff indeed, fail when their load limit is exceeded. The failure mode is treacherous; they simply snap without the usual deflection that a more limber pole might show, and therefore they give little notice of their imminent failure.

Weight is important because, after all, we have to carry these wretched things around with us all the time. And since the strength of a pole depends largely on its area cross-section, it follows that we gain a bit by using a thicker pole made of a lighter wood than a thinner pole made of a heavier wood. So the heaviest (or densest) wood isn't usually the best wood.

Finally, we give high marks for stability, which is a wood's ability to stay in the shape you give it when you mill it. Once you have a nice straight pole, you shouldn't have to worry about whether it will still be nice and straight when you take it out of the garage for the next tourney. Changes in moisture and temperature will want to make parts of the wood swell or shrink, but a well-behaved pole will shrink or swell evenly throughout its length, and equally on both sides, thereby continuing to be straight. Alder, an otherwise desirable wood, suffers from a lack of stability.

In a perfect world, the only forces a center pole would see would be perfect compression loads, bearing straight down on the top of a vertical pole. In this same world, the only loads a ridgepole would see would be bending loads, from the weight of the tent fabric. And the tent would magically go from a flat-on-the-ground state to a fully-set-up state. But the reality is that through the process of setting up the tent, some poles see a lot more stress, unevenly applied, than they'd see in their perfectly loaded state. And a center pole can expect to be leaned on, or run into, at some point in its long life. So we have to allow for a heftier pole than a simple load analysis would specify.

For information on specific kinds of woods, I refer you to the *Woodworking Factbook* by Donald G. Coleman (1966, Robert Speller and Sons), which describes several types of woods according to their properties. In my library I have several other books giving pretty much the same information, but this one gives you the most comprehensive rundowns of the various species of wood and their properties, and the most lucid explanations of what it all means. I'm not reproducing those lists here, because they mention many varieties of woods that may not be commonly available where you happen to be (especially if you aren't in North America). But with the following information, you should be able to describe to your lumber source what you're looking for, and have it recommend an equivalent wood available in your area at a price you can afford.

For my own center poles and ridgepoles, I use Douglas fir (not a true fir, but a pine), a wood commonly available in the western US. Its weight is moderate, but it ranks high in stiffness and bending strength, and it's readily available and cheap. Its stability is only moderate, but I've found that by paying more, you can get six-foot billets of "clear" (knotless) wood that are very consistent in grain and therefore reasonably stable. I join two of these lengths with sleeving to make my twelve-foot poles. Douglas fir is fairly easy to mill.

You can use a two-by-four with a knot or two in it for a ridge-pole, if you take care to orient the piece so that the knots are on top, and therefore under compression.

Those in the eastern US can use southern yellow pine, which has properties equivalent to Douglas fir.

What size to use? As a rule of thumb, I use an octagonal section of 2.25" diameter (measured along the flats), with a cross-sectional area of 4.2 square inches, for my round tents up to ten feet in diameter at the eave, and in all the ovals I've made. (Unlike the rounds, the center poles of the ovals carry only the weight of the roof, with the side poles supporting the weight of the sides. So this size seems to be plenty strong.) For the larger rounds, I go to a 2.5" diameter (again measured across the flats) with a cross-section of 5.2 square inches. These poles are typically between 11' and 12' long; if yours are going to be longer, increase the cross-section proportionately.

For comparison purposes, a 2" x 2" (which actually measures 1.5" x 1.5") has a cross-sectional area of 2.25 square inches, and a 2" x 4" (which actually measures 1.5" x 3.5") has cross-section of 5.25 square inches. Does this mean I could replace my bigger center poles with two-by-fours, and save myself a bunch of money? Well, no, because while a two-by-four would have plenty of stiffness in one direction, along the longer dimension, it would have much less in the perpendicular dimension. And a two-by-four would be far less stable, a fact you can confirm by going to a lumber yard and seeing exactly how few of their two-by-fours are actually reasonably straight.

For my shorter poles for all my tents, and for the longer poles of my sunshades, I use yellow poplar, another wood common in the US. At first glance, it doesn't seem a likely candidate it ranks only "moderate" in stiffness and bending strength. But where it shines is in stability and ease of milling. And its lightness (although nominally a hardwood, it's about the weight of white pine) allows me to go with an octagonal diameter of 1.75" (again, measured along the flats), which gives enough stiffness for even the center poles of the sunshades. Finally, because poplar tends to grow tall and straight, it's not too hard to find billets of the length needed to make tent poles. You have to be careful, though, that the grain is straight and true throughout the billet. A poplar pole cut across the grain will look fine, mill well and stay straight due to its inherent stability, but will still fail when subjected to great load.

127

I like Douglas fir and poplar not only for their suitability but also because they are "farmed" specifically for use in lumber, and are therefore renewable. By contrast, most hardwoods of sufficient size and length for tent poles come from old growth that will take scores of years to be replaced.

Oak and maple, if you can find them in useable lengths, make pretty good poles, but they don't rate very high in stability, so again you have to pay particular attention to consistency of grain. I should point out at this juncture that you should steer clear of wood where you have heartwood and sapwood in the same piece; with few exceptions (poplar is one of them) there is a dramatic difference in their properties, notably in stiffness and stability, so a pole made from this billet will probably give you trouble down the line.

By all means, buy your wood from a mill or lumberyard that understands what you'll be using it for. Unless you really, truly trust them, be sure to hand-pick your stock for straightness, even grain, and lack of knots. And, once you've got the pole the way you want it, finish it immediately so it stays that way.

How to set up a table saw for octagonal poles

Let's say you have nice, square poles, but you want to have octagonal poles instead. (Octagonal poles are much easier to handle and much less painful to run into if you're careless.) You don't have to deal with measurements and mathematics to set your table saw's fence for the right amount of material to be removed for a perfect octagon. All you have to do is follow the steps, as illustrated in Figure 37, below:

First, raise your saw blade to its highest position and then lean it over to 45 degrees. Hold your square pole stock so that it's flush with the saw blade and touching the saw table, and then slide your fence over until it touches the pole stock. That's where you want your fence, so lock it down and then lower the saw blade to a safer level.

Step two shows the first pass. When

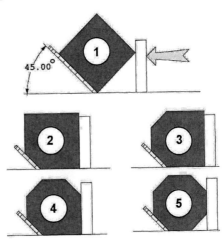

Figure 37. Setting up a table saw for octagonal poles

you rotate the wood for steps three to five, rotate the top of the stock toward the fence; that is, rotate it clockwise if your saw blade is to the left of the fence, as shown, or counter-clockwise if your saw blade is to the right of the fence and leaning the opposite direction from the illustration. (That way, you can continue using your featherboard to hold the wood in position. It also ensures that you have more stock against the table fence and the table until the last cut is made. (You do use a featherboard, don't you? If you don't know what a featherboard is, you'd better learn before tackling this project on a table saw).

A center-finding tool

Have you ever tried to determine the center of the end of a pole, so you could drill a hole for a spike? Not the easiest thing to do, but with this little tool it's a snap. You can buy one commercially, or you can make one like the one illustrated below. With it, you can accurately locate the center of any pole or dowel up to about three inches in diameter. What's more, it will work whether the pole is round, square, or octagonal. (If it's hexagonal, though, you're out of luck.)

Figure 38. A center-finding tool

The one I use consists of three pieces: two blocks of ¾" wood, about three inches square, and a single triangular piece of paneling. The triangular piece is cut with corner angles of ninety degrees and forty-five degrees. To assemble it, simply glue the two blocks together so that they form a perfect ninety-degree angle, using a combination square or equivalent tool for a reference. Then glue the triangular piece to the end of this assembly as shown by Figure 35, with the one of the short sides flush with the face of one of the blocks, and the long face accurately lined up on the intersection of the inner faces.

To fine-tune it, put a pole into the crotch formed by the two blocks, push it up against the triangular piece, and run a pencil along the angle across the end of the pole, as shown in Figure 36. Then turn the pole 180 degrees, and mark the line again. If the two lines coincide, great ... you're finished. If they don't, it's

Figure 39. The center-finding tool in use

because the plate was not accurately lined up with the junction of the two blocks, or the width of the pencil point itself hasn't been taken into account. To correct this, sand the edge of the panel a wee bit, and mark the two lines again. If the lines are moving closer together, you're on the right track, so keep sanding until they coincide. If you find that the lines are moving farther apart, you can either build up the edge with tape, or simply remove the triangular plate and re-glue it so that it can avail itself of your adjustment process.

Do the lines now coincide when the pole is rotated halfway? Then you're in business. To use the piece on your intended pole, lay the pole in the angle, just as you did during the calibration process. Draw the line across the top of the pole. Now rotate the pole ninety degrees and draw another line. The point where the two lines intersect is the exact center of the pole.

A line-boring tool

When I had to make a lot of poles with spikes in the top, I found it to be a real trial to line up the drill so that the hole goes accurately down the center of the pole. It seemed impossible to hold the drill so accurately that the hole (and consequently the spike) didn't end up leaning one way or another. "There has to be a better way," I thought to myself. About the only tools on the market that could do line boring were those specialty woodworking rigs like the Shopsmith and similar multi-purpose lathes, and the prices of these tools put them out of my reach. So I had to get clever.

This handy tool was made from one of those drill press stands that accommodate a hand

Figure 40. A shop-built line boring drill

130

drill. This one was designed for a ½" drill, so it was bigger than the standard ones. What sold me on this one, though, was the fact that it could drill holes up to 3" deep, which is how deep I set the pins that go into the ends of the dowels. I picked it up at our local used tool emporium for fifty bucks ... and that included the drill.

To modify the drill press stand, I simply removed the pedestal (which required loosening one set screw and pulling it off) and devised a pair of brackets to hold the pipe that forms the (formerly) upright stand of the drill press. I said "formerly" because as you see, the whole device now lays on its side, so as to accommodate poles of any length. The poles themselves are held in a cradle consisting of two holders, one of which you see in the picture. The other cradle is mounted about three feet to

Figure 41. Another view of the line borer

the right of the visible one, and serves mainly to preserve the alignment of the pole with respect to the drill, but doesn't do a very good job of physically supporting poles longer than about four feet long. For that, I usually employ one of those adjustable stands you can by at just about any woodworking supply or tool store.

Obviously, when the pole is resting in its cradle, the bottom of the pole is going to be in roughly the same place regardless of its thickness, but the center of the pole (where you want to bore the hole) will vary in its height above the table depending on the thickness of the pole. So there had to be some method of regulating the height of the drill above the table.

I originally made the brackets to be adjustable, so that I could loosen and tighten them at will and thereby adjust the height of the drill off the table, but the adjustments wouldn't stay locked in under the weight and motion of the drill. It eventually dawned on me that there were only a few diameters of poles I needed to deal with, and there was therefore no need for the mechanism to be infinitely variable. So I devised pieces of wood of varying thicknesses to put between the drill and the table – a different thickness for each pole diameter I use. When I set up the jig for a particular pole diameter, I select the piece with the proper thickness to raise the height of the drill to the

131

correct elevation. The drill slides along on top of this spacer, with the drill's own weight keeping it at the right level.

The device has now been used to make hundreds of poles and requires no maintenance except for keeping the sliding mechanism slippery, which I achieve with silicone spray, and the occasional replacement of the drill bit itself.

There are two other details that might not be apparent at first glance. First, I've installed an adjustable hose clamp on the main shaft of the stand. This device acts as a stop, so that all the holes have identical depths without me having to measure each one. Second, the bed of the line-boring tool is designed to be laid on my workbench and be clamped to it by the side and end vises. When I'm done, I just unclamp the jig and lift the whole affair off the bench, liberating the bench top for other projects.

Making Poles Out of Other Materials

For some people, wood isn't practical because of its weight, expense, or whatever, and they seek alternatives. They can use steel pipe with good results, if they understand that steel is more plastic (less stiff) than wood and that they'll need to use a diameter great enough to provide the necessary stiffness. And the larger diameter usually means more weight.

Some sorts of conduit work well and are readily obtained. But don't use EMT (thinwall) tubing. This stuff is not really designed for stiffness; in fact, it's designed to be easily bent, because electricians have to bend it all the time.

Similarly, I'd stay away from PVC or other plastics. Again, they're not designed to carry any load, and they tend to get brittle over time. I've only seen one design that I'd consider successful ... a friend of mine named Randy Yamamoto made a "yurt-like" structure using lots of PVC pipe like Tinker Toy pieces. The tent stood up to winds well enough, but the tent flexed greatly and creaked loudly, leaving its inhabitants sleepless and anxious.

If you need a pole that's really lightweight, go to whoever sells hang gliders and ultralights (or microlights, as they're called in British-speaking parts of the world) in your area and see if they have any damaged or bent aluminum spars on hand that they'll sell you for the price of the scrap. These can usually be straightened and sleeved (or otherwise reinforced) so you can use them. (The reason the original owner couldn't do this is because it would have affected the weight distribution and handling properties of the aircraft ... not a problem, in your case.) It's fairly easy to get this stuff in different diameters, allowing you to make as few or as many breakdown joints as you wish. You'll want to cover them with paint or wood-grained contact paper, though, or otherwise disguise their non-period provenance.

People have expressed a certain amount of concern about whether metal poles are more conducive to lightning strikes than wood poles. I can only say that lightning pretty much does as it pleases, regardless of the composition or relative height of the pole. It would seem that it's really not of great concern unless you're far and away the highest tent in the encampment *and* you have a metal pole *and* the gods happen to be angry with you

Afterward

Children make the best correspondents, Mark Twain wrote, because "they tell all they know, then stop." In this book there are undoubtedly some places where I have failed to tell all I know, and others where I have failed to stop, but I have done my best.

Nobody knows everything. The only recommendation for the stuff in this book is that most of it has come from my thirty years of industrial sewing experience, including close to twenty years of designing tents, making tents, and living in tents. Others may have had different experiences, and consequently offer different advice. So think of this book as a starting point for your education on tents, and learn from as many people's experience as possible, not just mine.

Comments are always welcome. You can write me at:

John LaTorre
P.O. Box 13322
Sacramento, CA 95813-3322

Appendix A: Sources

for Plans and Further Information

Books:

The Known World Handbook
Pavilions of the Known World (The *Complete Anachronist* # 26)
    Contain articles on tentmaking, with some plans. Both are available from the SCA Marketplace at:
Society for Creative Anachronism
P.O. Box 360789
Milpitas, CA 95036-0789
Telephone: (800) 789-7486
https://secure.sca.org/cgi-bin/stockclerk/index

Period Pavilions - The Book! by Coryn Weigle
    A valuable reference for tentmakers, but hard to find. As of the summer of 2006, this book was described on their web site as "out of print, currently being revised and expanded." Available from:
Mediaeval Miscellanea
6530 Spring Valley Drive
Alexandria, VA 22312-2131   USA
(703) 642-1740
(http://www.mediaevalmisc.com/)

Web sites:

Tanya Guptill's ***Medieval Pavilion Resources***
(http://www.currentmiddleages.org/tents/)
Along with almost all the stuff on tentmaking found on the Rialto, she also has these pages of special interest:
Make Your Own Mini Pavilion, by Tanya Guptill
How to Make a Dormered Armoring Pavilion, by Valerie Lilley
A Viking A-Frame Style Pavilion, by M. "Kathryn" Ballard)

Pavilion Information from House Greydragon
(http://www.greydragon.org/pavilions/)
Features detailed construction plans and notes for a hub-and-spoke"pavalino"

David Friedman's ***Building a Conjecturally Period Pavilion***
(http://www.pbm.com/~lindahl/cariadoc/conjecturally_period_pavilion.html)

Max & Mickel's Easy, No-bake Pavilion
(http://www.sacoriver.net/~freegate/Pavilion.html)
A simplified approach to making a tent

Stefan's Florilegium
(http://www.florilegium.org/)
Mark Harris's compendium of all things medieval and SCA-oriented, with numerous articles on tents and tentmaking; look under "Shelter"

Dragonwing
(http://midtown.net/Dragonwing/)
The author's own web site, occasionally updated with new articles on tentmaking that supplement this book

Web sites, being as ephemeral as they are, may not be functioning by the time you visit them. However, a search using your favorite search engine will probably turn them up if you look them up by title or subject matter. Many of them also have links pages, allowing you to get to just about any site from any other site.

Appendix B: How to Make a "BC" Type Sunshade

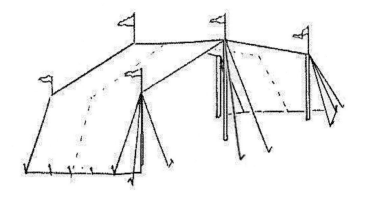

Figure 42. The "BC" Sunshade

This versatile sunshade is seen in SCA encampments over much of the American West, and increasingly in other places as well. It's very stable in winds, easy to set up, and reasonably rain-resistant as well. The original was designed by Dr. Fred Hollander (known in the SCA as Duke Frederick of Holland or simply "Flieg"), but subsequent research suggests that he had essentially re-invented what was a sixteenth or seventeenth century design. His first one was much longer and lower than the present design; when someone remarked that it looked like a Klingon battle cruiser, it acquired its present nickname of the "BC." In its most basic form, it consists of two or three lengths of 60"-wide cloth sewn together at the selvages, with the ends hemmed and reinforcements added to what will be the center ridge and wherever poles or stake ropes go through the fabric. Three panels are really the maximum; any more than this creates too much "sail area" and makes the entire structure more unstable. If a deeper sunshade is desired, it's better to make two sunshades of equal length and link them together, with the rear poles of the first sunshade doing double duty as the front poles of the rear sunshade. You'll still have a gap between the two sunshades, but this is desirable since the gap helps to vent the wind loads and thereby keep the two sunshades aerodynamically independent. Another benefit of using two linked sunshades is that it makes your camping arrangement more flexible ... if it's just you camping, bring a two-panel sunshade. If you've got friends, bring a three-panel sunshade. If you have a big household or need the space for a serious party (sounds oxymoronic, but you know what I mean), bring both sunshades and link them together to form a structure twenty-five feet deep. Some of you may remember Flieg's encampment at the Thirty Year Celebration, which consisted of four or five of these things strung together to form a Great Hall.

Figure 43. Two sunshades set up in tandem

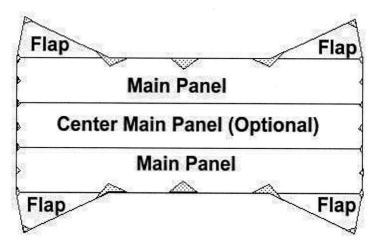

Figure 44. General plan of the sunshade (not drawn to scale). The shaded areas indicate reinforcement patches

Sewing the cover

I'm going to give you specifications for a 10' x 20' sunshade, the kind I most often make. Flieg's are usually larger (typically 15' x 30'), because his encampments are larger, and you can adjust the dimensions to suit you. By adding a center panel (which necessitates one more center pole), a 15' x 20' sunshade can be built with the same instructions, but you may want to add more patches for stake loop reinforcements and additional reinforcement for the third center pole.

The material I use is a 60" cotton-polyester twill about six or seven ounces in weight. I've used pure cotton and pure polyester as well, but found that these fabrics don't perform as well. The pure cotton is very stretchy and will distort much more over time than the cotton-poly blend. Some cotton content is important, though, since the cotton swells when damp, making the fabric less porous. The material isn't waterproof, and a hard rain will mist through it and there will inevitably be some seepage in rainy weather. But if the sunshade is properly pitched, most of the water will run down the inside of the fabric to the ground without dripping on the stuff underneath.

A truly waterproof material has an additional disadvantage of not letting any air pass through its fabric. The result of this lack of porosity is a much more effective wind-catching effect. This is why sailmakers have forsaken natural cloth for tightly-

141

woven polyester and other synthetic stuff, which they then treat heavily with resin or plastic to make it as impervious to air passage as they humanly can. They want more wind-catching efficiency in their products, but you don't. You want material that vents loads, not passes them along to the frame.

Stay away from nylon altogether. Although a nylon sunshade packs up small and is very strong and water-proof, it's so transparent to ultraviolet rays that it's quite possible to get a nasty sunburn while underneath it.

I do not recommend going over about eight ounces for your cloth. The additional weight really does nothing except add more weight to the poles and to the baggage we have to carry around. Two of the advantages of this design are its light weight and its minimum structure for the area it covers, and it would be a real shame to nullify these traits by using a heavy cloth. It also makes the cover much more difficult to sew.

If you've got some 48" wide cloth that will fit the bill, you can use three panels of that width instead of two panels of the 60" wide stuff. Four panels of 48" wide stuff will take the place of three panels of the 60" wide stuff.

This design also includes flaps (also called "elephant ears") to regulate wind and draft and help minimize the "wind tunnel" effect you get by having so much cloth open at the front and back and staked down at the sides. While these aren't strictly needed, at least on the smaller models, they add to the practicality of the design.

For a two-panel sunshade using 60" wide cloth, you'll need about 23 yards of fabric for the main body and patches, plus 5-1/2 yards for the flaps. For a three-panel sunshade, add another 10-1/2 yards.

For a three-panel sunshade using 48" cloth, you'll need about 33-1/2 yards for the main body and patches, plus 7 yards for the flaps. For a four-panel sunshade, add another 10-1/2 yards.

If you're wise, you'll order a little extra (like 10% more) to compensate for any errors that your cloth vendor might have made when measuring the cloth for sale.

Cut the main panels first, to be sure you have enough continuous cloth off the roll to form each panel. There are two ways to cut them. The first way, if you have a lot of space to cut and pin them up, is to cut each panel to a length of 364" (30' 4"). Maybe you work in an office building that has long hallways, where they won't mind you coming in after hours. (A friend of mine used to work at AT&T and used their hallways late at night to lay out sails.)

But if you're like me, with a cutting area that is only 24 feet long (or less), listen to Secret Trick #1: instead of cutting out one long panel, cut out two short ones. To be precise, they are each 15' 2", plus 12" for a seam allowance, for a total length of 16' 2" (or 194"). This has three benefits for me:

1. I can fit the panels on my cutting table with space all around.
2. With half panels, I can sew each half of the sunshade separately, and join them at the ridge at the last step. I'd rather assemble and sew two shorter seams than one long seam. Your experience may differ, but that's what mine has taught me.
3. You can use shorter pieces of fabric. Sometimes it's hard to get a good continuous thirty feet out of bargain cloth, what with thread flaws, splices, and so on. Shorter panels give you more latitude to cut around the bad stuff. Stuff too short for the main panels can be used for the flaps, patches, and other uses. (Another hint: order about six extra yards of cloth, and you'll have enough excess to discard the half-panel with the splice and make another.)

But doesn't that necessitate another seam along the ridge? Well, yes, but the top of the sunshade gets a lot of tension, so it has to be reinforced anyway, either with a strip of webbing, or a pocket with a rope in it, or with extra layers of the cloth itself. With the two-halves method, the ridge seam itself acts as the reinforcement. (I suppose you could call that benefit number four.)

Since I sew the ridge seam to be eight inches wide, each panel needs to be one foot longer to provide material for the seam allowance.

If you elect to use a single panel 30' 4" long, you might consider cutting it 20" longer so you can reinforce the ridge with a "false seam" ten inches wide, to provide the same reinforcement against stretch. That way, you won't have to sew webbing onto the ridge. "False seams" are explained in Chapter 14.

To make the flaps, roll out your cloth about eight feet. Along the selvage, draw a line two inches away from the selvage. This is your hem allowance. Along this line, make a mark two inches from the end of the cloth. We'll call this mark "A." Make another mark 94" from the first mark, along the line. This will be mark "B." Now make another mark along the line 10" from mark "A," still along the line. From this mark, measure across the cloth 44" and make another mark at that point. This is mark "C." When you connect marks "A," "B," and "C," you should have a triangle with each leg measuring 94" and the bottom measuring a tad over 45." You've already got the hem allowance for the first long side (that's the two-inch border between line A-B and the edge of

143

the cloth). Now draw a 2" hem allowance for the bottom and a 2" seam allowance for the remaining long side, and cut the panel out.

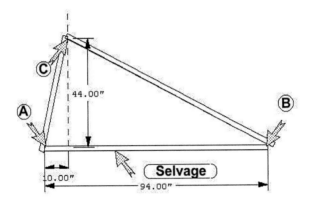

Figure 45. A schematic of the flap panel

Using this panel as a template, cut out three more panels just like it, marking point "B" on each one, but don't draw the other lines.

Cut out your reinforcements with the remaining material. You'll need six patches that are 20" square, which you'll be folding artfully to form the pole grommet reinforcements, plus enough patches to reinforce where the stake loop grommets will be going. These last patches are 10" square. For a two-panel sunshade, you'll need ten patches; for a three panel, make fourteen patches; and for a four-panel, eighteen patches If you aren't using the flaps in your design, subtract four of these smaller patches from the tally. You'll also need four patches 10" x 20" for the bottom corners of the flaps (if you're using flaps) or the corners of the sunshade (if you're not.

If you're using flaps in your design, you'll also need four pieces of material, 2" wide and 40" long, cut directly along either the warp or the fill of the cloth, but not on the bias.

Now to begin sewing. I usually sew the flaps to the main panels first. To do this, I make a mark 96" from the end of the panel along the selvage. Now I lay the flap onto the main panel, lining mark "B" on the flap with the mark I just made on the main panel and the bottom of the flap. I use the cut edge of the flap, not the selvage edge, when I'm forming this seam. You have to be careful not to put any tension on the flap at this seam, since, being cut somewhat on the bias, it will be more than happy to stretch beyond the 96" allotted to it. (There's a reason why we're not using the other long edge of the flap, where the selvage is, and I'll tell you the reason by and by.)

144

Sew the pieces together with a flat-fell seam. (See Chapter 14 if you don't know what that is. In fact, it would be wise to review the whole chapter, just so you understand the theory behind some of these patches and seams.)

Once the flaps are on, you sew the main panels together. I use the same flat-fell seam, although I suppose you wouldn't need to if you were using the full width of the cloth, and if the cloth has a true selvage (which doesn't fray). But I think the flat-fell seam adds a little strength as well.

Those of you who are using the single long panels will have to add the ridge reinforcement -- webbing, rope-in-pocket, false seam, whatever -- once all the panels have been sewn into one piece. Those who use the half-panel method will make a flat-fell seam, eight inches wide. (I find it easiest to form the seam entirely with pins and, with all folds in place, secure the seam with four stitch lines, removing the pins as I go. I guess that would make the seam something other than a true flat-fell, in which you first run one stitch line, then fold, and lastly run the other stitch line.)

Those with wider sunshades (three-panel for the 60"-cloth people or four-panel for the 48"-cloth people) will want to put another reinforcement directly on the ridge reinforcement, at the midpoint of the sunshade. This reinforcement is for the third center pole that the wider sunshades require. I usually use a square of 2" seat-belt webbing for this reinforcement, but you can use more cloth, or leather, or something else.

Now trace a hem line all around the sunshade, two inches in from the edge of the cloth. You'll be folding the edge to this line, then folding again at the line itself, to form a hem one inch wide with the edges of the cloth inside.

To make the patches, take the square of material and fold it point-to-point, forming a triangle. Fold it once again to form a smaller triangle. The cuts in the material should now be along the base of the triangle. The base of the triangle should be positioned on the hem line you just drew in the last step, so they go inside the hem of the sunshade, where they won't fray. The six larger triangles are to reinforce the area around the poles. The four for the side poles will go right at the top of the flap panel (96" from the end of the panel, remember); you'll have to trim them a little so they go around the angle formed by the main panel and the flap. The remaining two large patches go at each end of the ridge, where the center poles will go through the cloth.

The smaller patches are formed the same way, and are positioned at each seam in the main body of the sunshade, and also in the middle of each panel. Therefore, they should be 24" or 30" apart (depending on the width of the cloth you're using. The patches that go where the main body and a flap are seamed together will need to be trimmed to suit the slight angle formed there.

The 10"x20" patches for the flap corners are folded once, to form a 10"x10" square, and again to form a triangle. In this case, the shorter sides of the triangle are positioned at the hem line, leaving only the longest edge exposed when the hem is formed. Again, you'll have to do some trimming. Since this point is a high-stress area, I also put a piece of light webbing there, usually hiding it underneath the patch.

Before hemming up the sunshade, there's one more Secret Trick I'll share with you. The bottom of the flap is cut on the bias, and would stretch abnormally if we didn't do something about it. This is what the extra 40" strips of material are for. You cut these to 2" wide and oriented them so that either the warp threads or the weft (or fill) threads go all the way along them. These strips won't stretch very much. Sailmakers call this sort of reinforcement "tabling" and add it to a cloth border to give it more resistance to stretch (as opposed to a bias tape, which protects the edge from fraying but does absolutely nothing to control stretch). Pin or baste the strips to the bottom of the flap panel, so they will be sewn into the hem itself. With these two strips sewn into the hem, the hem won't stretch. In fact, you've now controlled stretch along each edge of the flap with the rein-forcement sewn into the bottom hem, one of the long sides sewn into the main body, and the remaining long side oriented so it runs along the warp of the cloth itself.

Now you can sew the hem around the sunshade. I also add a square of that 2" seat-belt webbing at each point where one of the frame poles goes through the fabric, on top of the patches already there. Is this overkill? Yeah, probably, but since I warrant my sunshades for five years, the extra reinforcement greatly adds to my peace of mind. Most of the home-sewn sunshades omit this last reinforcement, and most of them do just fine.

The last step is to install grommets. I use fairly large ones (#3 spur) where the poles go through the fabric, because this allows me to use a 3/8" rod at the end of the pole, and also because large grommets do a better job of spreading load than smaller grommets do. At the stake loop patches, #3 spur grommets will allow you to use 1/4" rope for your stake loops. To make these loops, cut a piece of 1/4" rope to a length of 16", and the ends together with a simple knot. Pass the loop you just formed through the grommet, and voila! If you're using 3/8" "wire spike" stakes to stake the fabric to the ground, you can dispense with the loops altogether and run the stakes through the grommet instead.

Making the frame and setting it up

Constructing the Framework

For your sunshade, you'll need four side poles, each seven feet long. (The dimensions are not very critical.) You'll also need some ten-foot poles ... two if you've made the shallower version of the sunshade (using two panels of 60" cloth or three panels of 48" cloth), and three if you have the deeper version.

Note on center poles: If you're building a frame for a wider sunshade, like 25' or 30' wide, your center poles should be 11' long rather than 10' long. This will give you better tension and rain-shedding ability.

In any of the designs, you can use 2" x 2" "dimensional" lumber (actually 1-½" x 1-½") or 1 5/8" "closet round" dowel for the side poles. For the center poles, I would go with something heavier, like a hardwood of equivalent cross section or (if you're stuck with softwood) something like 2" x 4" "dimensional" lumber (actually 3-½" x 1-½"). For more information on recommended woods, check out Chapter 18 on tent poles.

Now finish the poles, as directed in Chapter 2.

All of the sunshades that come from the Dragonwing factory utilize fourteen stakes to stake the fabric to the ground, all 12" long. We also use 12" stakes for the eight side-pole ropes, and four 16" stakes for the center-pole guy ropes. All our stakes are the forged ones made from 1/2" square stock. If your stakes aren't up to these specifications, and you're building a three-panel sunshade, you should use more stakes on the skirt of the sunshade ... no more than 30" or so apart (except for the ear flaps, which are fine with a single stake because they don't contribute as much to the stability of the sunshade).

For the 12" stakes, I recommend using the 12" wire spike stakes that I described in Chapter 3. For the 16" stakes, you could use lengths of "rebar" or 1/2" square or round stock with one end bent over to retain the rope. Grind the other end to a point, and you're in business.

You'll also need some 3/8" rod stock to finish the poles. Each pole will need a six-inch piece. (If you wish, you can use it to mount a pennant pole with an appropriately-sized socket at its base.) Wrap the end of each pole with filament tape and drill a hole in the top end that's

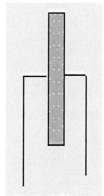

Figure 46. The pole spike in place

147

three inches deep. Cut the rod stock to length, round off the ends, and insert the stud into the pole. (See figure 46). At our shop, we glue the rod in with epoxy or a urethane glue. Finally, apply the finish of your choice.

Find the rope, and a knife. Cut two lengths, each 30' long. Find the midpoint of each length and tie a loop there. We'll call this the "fixed" loop because it doesn't adjust. At each end of the rope segment, install a rope slider or tie a slip knot into each end, and slide the knot so the distance from the fixed loop to each end of the rope is about 12' long.

When we make rope sets at our factory, we mark these center-pole rope assemblies with a little piece of ribbon in the fixed loop, so we can tell them apart from the other rope assemblies. We advise you to scrounge up some yarn or ribbon and do likewise, or devise your own method of telling these rope sets apart from the others.

Now cut four lengths, each 25' long. For each length, find the midpoint, and tie a fixed loop there. Finally, finish each end as you did the others, with a slip knot or a slider. Adjust the loops so that these rope segments are about 8' long. These ropes will be for your side poles.

Setting Up the Sunshade

There about as many ways to set up this sunshade as there are people setting them up. The methods described below are based on the "fast up" tent pitching method. It's the only method I use nowadays, because it reduces the time spent actually raising the fabric and therefore results in less possibility of damaging it (or yourself!). The technique consists of laying the sunshade on the ground and then measuring where the stakes go, using either the tent poles or guide knots on your guy ropes to determine the appropriate distance. Then the rope ends are slipped on the stakes, the pole spikes are inserted into their respective holes in the sunshade, and the loop of the guy ropes slipped over the spike ... all while the sunshade is still on the ground. Then the poles are raised. This technique has two advantages: it's much easier for one person to do, and it reduces to an absolute minimum the interval from the time the sunshade is lying on the ground until the moment that it's up and guyed.

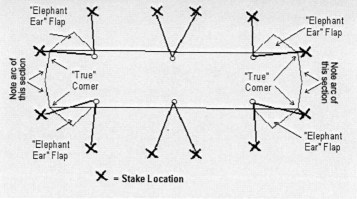

Figure 47. General location of stakes for the sunshade

Decide where you want to pitch the sunshade, and lay out the fabric there. Remember that the guy ropes will project about five feet out from the sunshade, and be sure to allow for that if you need to leave a walkway clear out front. Your "frontage dimension" (from one side to the other) will be about ten feet less than the space the sunshade takes up when it's flat on the ground.

Keeping the sunshade on the ground, slip all the pole studs through their respective grommets (except for the center-most center pole, if you have a three-panel sunshade) and put the loops of the ropes onto the studs (remember that the center pole ropes have little ribbons on the loops, right?). It is helpful, but not absolutely necessary, to have some sort of retaining device on the tops of the studs to keep the loops on the studs.

Now you can situate and place the stakes. There are two ways to determine the distance, as I mentioned earlier. Using the pole lengths as a guide is recommended for any sunshades that require three center poles, but the guide-knot method works well for the ones with only two center poles. We'll discuss the former method first.

Using the Poles to Position the Stakes

Unbundle the center pole ropes and lay them out so that they are at roughly a sixty degree angle from the sunshade. Lay one of the center poles alongside the rope, and use its length to determine where the stake goes. Drive the stake into the ground at that point. Set all four of these stakes, slip the guy rope loops over the stakes, and proceed to the corners.

The corner ropes go parallel and perpendicular to the front edge of the sunshade. You can use the length of the side poles to set the stakes, although you might want to subtract one foot (30 cm) from the length for those ropes that go parallel to the front edge of the sunshade. This is because when the sunshade is lifted, the tops of the side poles will be drawn closer to the center poles than they were on the ground, and all the stakes will end up the same distance from the poles. Set all eight stakes.

149

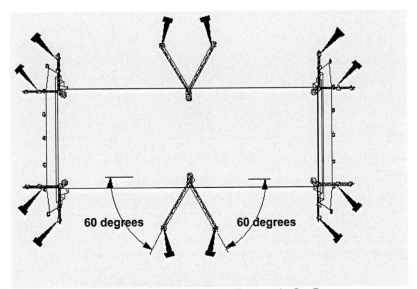

Figure 48. Locating the Stakes by Knots on the Guy Ropes

Using Guide Knots to Position the Stakes

This method described above sets out the stakes at an optimum distance, and gives each guy rope a 45° angle to the ground. However, the smaller sunshades can generally do with a steeper angle, since the loads they subject the guy ropes to aren't as great. And the steeper ropes present less of a tripping hazard. I've found through experience that one can safely go with a distance of five feet out for the center poles, and four feet out for the side poles. The second method requires tying a few knots in the guy ropes at those intervals. For the center pole guys, measure down five feet from the loop and tie a knot there. That knot is where you're going to drive the center pole stakes. To set the stake, slip the center pole's spike though its corresponding grommet in the sunshade and loop the guy rope's loop onto the spike. Then stretch the ropes out at a 60° angle from each other and the sunshade's edge, as shown in the sketch below. Drive the stakes into the ground next to the knot, and you'll know it's the right distance away. Set all four of these stakes and proceed to the corners.

Each of the corner ropes should have not one, but two guide knots: one at a three-foot interval, and one at a four-foot interval from the guy rope loop. This is because the stakes for the side ropes (the ones going parallel to the main body of the sunshade) have to be closer to the pole tops when the sunshade is on the ground. When the poles are raised, the peak in the roof will move

150

the side poles about a foot closer to the center poles than they were on the ground, and all the stakes will end up the same distance from the poles. Having two knots will allow you to use the same rope for either a side rope or a front-to-back rope, depending on which knot you use. (See the detail for the corner ropes and stakes, which is Figure 46.)

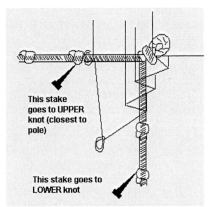

This stake goes to UPPER knot (closest to pole)

This stake goes to LOWER knot

Figure 49. Detail showing corner pole guide knots

So using the upper knots (the ones closest to the pole top) for the side ropes and the lower knots for the front-to-back ropes, locate where the stakes go. Drive the stakes in at these points, and slip the rope loops onto the stakes.

Raising the Poles and Staking Down the Sides

Now raise all the poles, starting with the side poles and then the center poles (including that center-most center pole if you have one). If the wind is strong, you should raise the windward poles first, then the leeward poles. As each pole is raised, the guy ropes will help stabilize it. When all the poles are up, adjust the guy rope lengths for tension and lack of wrinkles. In particular, pay attention to any sag between the center poles, and remove as much as you can by tensioning the center pole ropes. Then you can stake down the sides as described below.

When you stake down the sides, start with the loops at the "true" corners (not the loops at the elephant ears), as shown in Figure 42. Next, stake down the "elephant-ear" flaps if you wish. At the central stake loop at the base of the sunshade, pull the loop out (that is, away from the sunshade) as far as you can to impart maximum tension to the shade at that that point; this arc is also shown in Figure 42. If you don't do this, there will be a sag in the roof that will allow rainwater to pool and drip through the fabric. Yes, the loops will no longer be in a straight line with the corner loops; the resulting arc is what you want. Then put the stake in there. Do the same with the remaining stake loops. By pulling out on the loops this way, you greatly increase the fabric's tension and, consequently, its ability to shed water and resist luffing. On sunshades with three center poles, this step is especially crucial, because it's the resulting tension that keeps

151

the sunshade from lifting off the spikes when the wind picks up. (Under most wind conditions, you'll probably only have to use every other stake loop, but the ones in the center of the arc are critical, so never fail to use them.) Figures 50, 51, and 52, later in this section, show you why and how to perform this necessary but often overlooked step.

If there are several wrinkles in the top part of the sunshade, between the poles, then here's a troubleshooting guide:

First, be sure that the stakes are where they're supposed to be. If they're too close to the sunshade, you won't be able to get the guy ropes tight enough to properly tension the fabric.

If the poles on the "BC" sunshades are out of line with each other, or if the bottoms are staked out asymmetrically, you'll get a lot of funny diagonal wrinkles. The solution is to pull up one side of the sunshade's bottom, diddle with the adjustments on the ropes until the poles are all vertical and in line not only with each other but also with the staked-down bottom side. The wrinkles are always in the direction of the greatest tension, so you loosen the guy ropes attached to the poles on either end of the wrinkle, and tighten the other ropes attached to that section. Then stake down the last side. You can avoid a lot of this by raising all the poles first, adjusting the ropes so the "roof" part is all pretty and tight, and staking down the bottom last – first one side, then the other. For maximum tension, remember to stake down each side first at the corners – not at the flap (if there is one) but at the stake loop on the seam that runs from the top of the side pole to the ground. Then stake down the center, pulling outward as much as possible before you drive the stake in. Finally, stake down the remaining stake loops and the flaps.

If you have good tension between the center poles, and also between the side poles on each side, but you still have a lot of slack in the area between the side pole "shoulder" and the ridge, the sides need to be re-staked. Look at the sunshade in Figure 50. You'll see that the roof exhibits a great deal of slack. This is bad for two reasons. First, the sagging area is going to act as a rain catcher, eventually creating a puddle that will drip through on the inside. Second, if the wind picks up, there isn't going to be enough tension on the roof to keep it from lifting up off the central center pole, leaving the latter free to fall any which way it pleases.

Figure 50. Slack in sunshade roof

152

What causes this slack? As you can see in Figure 51, all the tent stakes on the side have been set in a straight line, aligned with the stretched out surveyor's tape.

Here's how to get rid of that slack. Stake down the two corners, getting good tension between them. Now grab the stake loop at the center of each side, and pull it outward as far as you can – at least six inches to a foot, depending on the size of the sunshade. Figure 52 show the arc in the line of stakes that this operation produces. You'll notice that the sag disappears like magic.

Figure 51. Bottom stakes in a line

Figure 52. Proper location of bottom stakes

Breaking down the sunshade is pretty much the reverse of the above procedure, with one exception. I drop the poles first, starting with the center poles and finishing with the side poles, to get the fabric on the ground and out of the wind. Then I remove the guy rope stakes, using the still-attached ropes to tell me where they are. Finally, I pull the remaining stakes up.

My favorite way to store the guy ropes is to fold them into wide loops, like a lasso, and then tie the loop in a loose overhand knot to keep the loops together.

Some people like to fold the sunshade neatly, but I prefer to stuff it back into the bag. According to sailing lore, this method keeps the cloth from getting creased in the same places all the time and therefore extends the life of the sunshade. It's also much easier for one person to do.

153

Index